DUTY BEYOND THE DESK

DUTY BEYOND THE DESK

The Journey of the Major

Written By:

Major (ret'd) Patrick Skeete

Publisher:
Aldon Enterprises
No.37 Hanson Heights, Dash Valley, St. George

PUBLISHER'S NOTES

Paperback Edition (6.25 x 9.25)
ISBN-978-976-95869-0-1

Other Editions: The Combermere Cadet (2004)

Book Design and Text Composition by
Grafixx 2 Inc: *info@grafixx2inc.com*

I dedicate this book to my parents,
the late Frederick and Marcia Skeete,

my wife Eartha St. Cyr-Skeete,

my children,
Gemma Grant, Alicia Skeete, Janelle Skeete,
Keitha St. Cyr and Earthon St. Cyr,
and my grandchildren.

Foreword

Colonel (ret'd) H.D. Maynard, SCM, ED, plsc

Former cadet of No. 3 Coy
Former teacher at Combermere

Former OC No. 3 Company (1971 - 1980) Former Chief of Staff, BDF (1999 – 2003)

The bold title of this absorbing and instructive work requires an explanation. It truly "captures the essence of what the story is about," as Patrick, himself, puts it. "Duty beyond the Desk," is written in the first person "because I wanted the reader to be aware that what I write about is what I experienced first-hand," Major Patrick Skeete boldly emphasizes. His intriguing volume which in the main deals with his personal involvement is the natural follow up to the pictorial review "The Combermere Cadet," also authored by Patrick. The concept, research and development of this effort required a great deal of dedication and commitment.

The various experiences which shaped his early life are all revealed to the reader. Patrick takes an in depth look at the social relations that obtained in the rural St. Peter village of Rose Hill in the 1950's, a place that is also the birth place of one of Barbados' former prime ministers, Mr. Owen Arthur. Day to day life is brought to the fore. The many games long lost or forgotten played by children of that era, the influence of his parents and other family members, along with primary school experiences are insights into the past. The very considerable importance of the teachers, clergy and church members of the period, rare visits made to places beyond the village, that like other rural villages of that time appeared to be isolated from the rest of Barbados, are also all richly portrayed. The coming of television, Patrick asserts, had a negative impact on village life of the period. This part of the work certainly builds on and adds to a growing collection of childhood memories brought back to life by Barbadian writers of our time.

Nonetheless, this ambitious volume is about more than childhood experiences and life in a rural village. It is also about life beyond Rose Hill, life at Combermere, his introduction to the Barbados Cadet Corps and his integration into the Combermere family.

On maturing, Patrick is now able to look wide and to build further on his experiences gained from camps in Dominica, St. Lucia, St Vincent and Guyana and on the entry of females into the Corps.

The development of a National Cadet Band, the expansion of the Corps to cover all secondary schools in Barbados, the development of the Sea Cadet Programme and other initiatives are all testimony to the work done by one who can justifiably be called the "pioneer of cadetting" in the latter part of the twentieth century and early part of the twenty-first century. The creation of a network of cadet officers was a significant development - a network that reached out from Barbados throughout the OECS countries, to Trinidad and Tobago, Cayman Islands, British Virgin Islands, Canada and the United Kingdom, all working together towards one common goal, that is the use of military discipline in the development of character. Punctuality, respect for authority, physical and mental endurance, teamwork and proper deportment are all stressed. These are considered vital elements of good citizenship.

In closing, a point raised by Major Skeete is important enough to bear repetition: "One aspect of the Canadian cadet system which we in Barbados could examine more closely is how they make use of their retired officers. They use creative ways to incorporate them into the system, where they continue to influence the development of the youth organization." If our people are indeed our most important resource, then perhaps we need to make use of the resource that is our retired elders.

It is my fervent hope that those who follow in his footsteps will faithfully continue this tradition of service to young men and women of Barbados, the region and the wider world.

I wish to thank you, Major Skeete for the extremely valuable and important work which catalogues the achievements, the many challenges and the disappointments which you encountered as you carried out your "duty beyond the desk" in an expanded Barbados Cadet Corps, in the latter years of the twentieth century and the early years of the twenty-first century. It is an engrossing, timely and pioneering work. It was a duty that required an effort that went beyond the desk.

Contents

Glossary of Abbreviations and Terms Used

BDF:	Barbados Defence Force
BCC:	Barbados Cadet Corps
Recce:	Reconnaissance / a site visit
Col:	Colonel
Lt. Col.:	Lieutenant Colonel
Cdr:	Commander
Lt Cdr:	Lieutenant Commander
LCdr:	Lieutenant Commander
Capt:	Captain
Lt:	Lieutenant
S/Lt:	Sub-Lieutenant
2 Lt:	Second Lieutenant
PCO:	Potential Cadet Officer
PO:	Potential Officer
OCdt:	Officer Cadet
UO:	Under Officer
CSUO:	Cadet Senior under Officer
CUO:	Cadet under Officer
CSM:	Company Sergeant Major
WO 1:	Warrant Officer Class 1
WO 2:	Warrant Officer Class 2
CQMS:	Company Quarter Master Sergeant
Sgt:	Sergeant
Cpl:	Corporal
L/Cpl:	Lance Corporal
NCO:	Non-Commissioned Officer
Pte:	Private
OC:	Officer Commanding
Star Levels:	*Star 1 Cadet, Star 2, Star 3 and Star 4.* These are levels of qualification for cadets in training. Cadets can earn stars numbering 1 to 4 over a four-year period.

On duty at my desk.

1

The End of a Career

Here I am, sitting at my desk relaxing before my final engagement on my last day in office. I continue to reflect as I have done over the past few days, as the events of my life flood my consciousness with memories too precious to keep tucked away - hidden from some young person seeking direction in life.

I am filled with mixed emotions as I recall eighteen years of memories at this desk and, indeed, my life before it came to represent so much. A small tear forms in the corner of my eye and with a sluggish motion, I brush it away. Did I do my very best? I think so.

We receive a baton from others and it is our duty to run the race with as much vigour and courage as we can muster, knowing that we cannot run forever.

It seems like only yesterday I was in the thick of things. Now I am passing the proverbial baton - relinquishing duty after 37 years of providing leadership for cadets.

In 1994, my first year at this desk, there were only three other workers and many empty rooms. Staff members now fill the entire building.

Ms. Cicely Drayton, the attendant, was one of the original staff members, and she is still here. We are the two longest serving members of staff at this location – the Barbados Cadet Corps Headquarters. Then there was a very efficient military clerk, Pte. Michelle Thompson, who is now a Colour Sergeant and works in another department of the Barbados Defence Force. Ms. Karen Crichlow was the first civilian clerk to work at Cadet Headquarters, and both she and Miss Drayton were extremely helpful to me.

Now, as I prepare to take my leave, we have fourteen staff members, a newly refurbished building with computers, air-conditioning, internet access, jeeps, a Land Rover, cars and a bus. What a contrast it is to my first day at work with only three staff members on payroll, one Land Rover and no air-conditioning nor computers.

My cupboard is crammed with documents, and my computer, which was not here eighteen years ago, contains years of information keyed and stored for posterity. What would we do now without computers? We started out with just a typewriter. If a document contained an error, we either salvaged it with "white out" liquid or tore it up and started over. Now with computers, we can make errors which are easily corrected and store the documents for later use. The example of the computer and the changes which resulted remind us that change is constant. The years go by and we come to the point where we have to say our "goodbyes" and move on to another phase of life.

It is with a feeling of utter satisfaction that I am finally closing this chapter of my life. The Cadet Corps and the interaction, the lives touched, the friendships, the long hours in office, in camps and other training activities, the many contacts and the experiences were all worth the effort.

Very often in life, we proceed without giving thought to that moment when we have to finally leave office. No one adequately prepares us for it. Very few training sessions are devoted to retirement issues. It is always seen as something in the distance, which we need not focus on when we are young and enterprising. But this could easily be a mistake. Retirement comes rather quickly and, if we are not prepared, it could be devastating. There is always a lingering desire to be "occupied." Having no occupation can lead to boredom and a range of other problems. In my case, thankfully, my life was not tied completely to the Cadet Corps. I am a member of the Church Board of the Berean Bible Church and I am also the Vice-Chairman of the Inter-School and Inter-Varsity Christian Fellowship. These are areas where I can continue to make a contribution.

Nothing in this world lasts forever and, if we live, we will come to that point. How we plan for it and how we handle it determine how we move forward.

The important thing in life is to know when it is time to move on. I have had an intense career with many exciting moments to recall, but there is that defining moment when it becomes clear that one has reached the zenith and life requires a change.

When someone retires, there are usually people who say that they are going to tap into your wealth of knowledge and information and will call on you when you leave. This is not always practical. However, it does allow for others in the workplace who fill the breach to forge ahead with their own plans. The secret for moving forward, therefore, as a retired person, lies in finding new avenues for sharing one's talents. Retirement, then, can be an exciting time, as one enters a new domain with certain unknowns.

The typical question asked by many people who heard that I was retiring was "What are you going to do now?" It was as though they could not conceive of the fact that one could have other interests besides work. They sometimes added "But you are a young man..," and in my mind, the words would ring out "Exactly! I am young enough to start a new life doing things at my own pace." Also, deep in my thoughts was a plan to spend time documenting my past for the sake of future generations.

Being in authority tends to grow on you and the loss of that importance could easily be a problem. This is not a concern for me. Military rank, social status and power have never mattered to me. For twenty-one years I held the post of Major in this new Cadet Officer/BDF Officer dispensation. It was one of the systemic problems which could easily lead to frustration. To continue to work very hard in circumstances where there were no prospects or opportunities for upward mobility, particularly because of how the system was set up, required much patience and self-sacrifice. Luckily, I never lost focus. While other officers from Barbados and overseas forces moved on from junior officer to Major and beyond, I remained in the same rank, although it sometimes meant becoming junior to many of whom I was initially senior. But to serve the greater good is what matters. There is always something bigger than self.

There were occasions when I received a call at this desk on Sundays, and I later asked myself, "Have I have become so predictable? Do people think that I don't have a life of my own?" Such was the nature of the job. Though the original intent was for me to work from 9:00 a.m. to 5:00 p.m., Mondays to Fridays, this time schedule became just a formality. To make the Cadet Corps function effectively, one needed to spend extra time at work.

What strange circumstances led me to this job? What strategies did I use? What was my vision? What challenges did I face? Who or what contributed to my success? Circumstances may be different in several countries, but there are some basic guidelines for duty beyond the desk which I want to share. As the first Cadet Executive Officer of a Cadet Corps, which is more than one hundred years old, I have an opportunity to share something unique, especially since I spent forty-two of those years assisting the cadets, mainly as an officer and also as a school teacher.

My brother-in-law, Wendell Haynes, who was a Cadet Under Officer of No. 2 Company, advised that, as a retiree, I should find some time to document the thinking process behind the activities which we conceptualized and executed in the Corps. My good friend and former colleague, Lieutenant Colonel Trevor Browne repeatedly reminded me that it was time to write a second book about the Cadet Corps. Eight years ago, when the Barbados Cadet Corps was celebrating its centenary, I wrote a book titled "The Combermere Cadet," which was the culmination of years of research into the history of Combermere Cadets.

At social events or chance meetings at the supermarket, former Prime Minister of Barbados, Mr. Owen Arthur, who headed the Defence Board at one time, would always encourage me to write a second book. He even hinted at the need to document what it was like growing up in our village, as he too grew up in my neighbourhood.

Initially, I deliberated about whether I should write about myself, because for all my life, I quietly did what was necessary, helping others without any fuss or fanfare. I was reminded that there are few people who are willing to sit and record history, and, that, because of my long involvement in the Cadet Corps, I had a responsibility to chronicle its activities.

This book gives the reader the rationale behind my actions and the motives of those with whom I worked. It also explains the methodology which we used in attempting to build strength of character in our young cadets. It is said that in Barbados, our people are our most important resource and, of course, the training must begin when they are young and capable of being molded.

In our culture, there is usually a lot of information and history locked away in the minds of people and it is only revealed when they lecture or chat with others. However, for the sake of those who come after us, we have an obligation to leave a record of life as it was in our time.

Early in 2014, Moonesh Dharampaul, a former Cadet from No. 4 Company, Ellerslie Secondary, spotted me as I was shopping in a mall and invited me to have tea or coffee with him. As we sat and chatted about the Cadet Corps, he revealed that he wanted to "give back" something to the Corps. He also asked the typical question about my retirement. I mentioned that I was writing an autobiography, and he called me later to say, "Sir - I have a title for you - Duty Beyond The Desk." I smiled, because it adequately captured the essence of what this story is about. I knew that I was meant to meet him that morning. My prayer for a suitable title for this book had been answered.

My thoughts go back to my early childhood, and to fully understand my role in life and what motivated me, it is necessary to take a trip with me, into the past, to see the various influences in my life.

2
The Importance of the Home Environment

The street in Rose Hill showing houses of my neighbours, June 2015

Naturally, there are many influences in one's life and, for me, the most important, are the home and family, the school, the church and the community.

Rose Hill, St. Peter, where I grew up, was a close-knit neighbourhood back in the late 1950s and 1960s. My parents, Frederick and Marcia Skeete, created the best possible circumstances for us as children. My siblings, Jennifer, Patricia and Steve and I were blessed to have such forward-thinking parents who believed strongly in the power of education. This was the period when free secondary education meant something special, since they themselves did not have that opportunity. Like any other parents in our village, their formal education was limited

Fred and Marcia Skeete (Parents of Author)

to primary school, but that education was very sound.

Our mother's profession brought the community to our home. She was a seamstress, and this meant that relatives and other members of the community were regular visitors to our home. This allowed us to interact with many people, although at times from a respectful distance, as children were not allowed to "mix in older people's business." They were to be "seen and not heard." Naturally, people became the center of our interest.

My father worked at the Barbados Transport Board for the greater part of his life, first as a conductor, later as an inspector and, finally, as pay master in the main office in Roebuck Street, St. Michael. However, in the earlier years, he joined the Barbados Volunteer Force and soon found himself training in Trinidad preparing for possible action in World War II.

Thankfully, the War ended before he was required to face up to the "supreme sacrifice" of laying down his life in battle. But this military training continued to be exhibited in how he cleaned our shoes, his upright stance and his military gait. Without even seeing him, some of our neighbours could tell from his rhythmic footsteps that is was Fred Skeete going home at night. He was a disciplinarian. If we were inclined to do something wrong, we learned that it was better to do it later in the day, because if it was done in the morning, we would have a long, miserable day to wait and think about what punishment we would receive. This was not to say that our mother did not have effective ways of disciplining us.

Parents have an influence on what we become, and I believe that my father's desire to serve his country as a soldier was replicated in me.

We grew up with limited resources, but we were very contented. We are all part of the Gilkes and Bend families from Rose Hill and surrounding areas, and the Skeete family from Rock Hall, St. Lucy.

Rose Hill was the typical Barbadian village, where many relatives lived in close proximity. My grandparents' house was on the opposite side of the road to ours. My maternal grandmother, Zulieka Gilkes (nee Bend), my grandfather Christopher Gilkes and our aunt, the late Cora Small (nee Gilkes), were all involved in our upbringing. Our uncle, Reverend Overton Gilkes, who is an Anglican Priest, lived overseas for a while and occasionally resided in Barbados. Our grandfather had grown up in Cuba and had come to Barbados as a teenager. We were aware that he could speak in Spanish. It is not surprising that I developed a love for Spanish and, in turn, my daughter Gemma also uses Spanish in her current job. It is part of our cultural heritage.

We spent the greater part of our summer vacations in Rock Hall, St. Lucy at the home of my father's uncle, Mr. Clifton Skeete, and his wife Cameron. It was a wonderful to spend time with our cousins, Gary, Carson, Douglas, Margaret, Jeffrey, Aileen, Pamela, Shirley and all the other family members who lived nearby. I particularly remember the love shown to us by my father's grandmother, "Mammy," who lived next door to his uncle. There was someone related to us in almost every house on that road.

Rock Hall, St. Lucy provided a nurturing environment in which everyone was his brother's keeper. The same could be said of Rose Hill, St. Peter, where older relatives in the neighbourhood kept us in check. We referred to some of these as "Great Aunts" - Aunt Manda, Aunt Millie and Aunt Baby Gilkes - who were the sergeants major in our lives. Their visits to our house would see us scampering to ensure that everything was in order and demonstrate that we were doing our household chores.

There was that extended family who cared and who felt that it was their job to help raise us as children. The saying, "It takes a village to raise a child," was very true then. We dared not let anyone see us engaging in any bad behaviour on the street. Indeed, young people of that era were subject to the discipline of the entire community. If a neighbour heard you utter a "bad" word, they not only scolded you, they would somehow relay a message to your parents before you got home, and then you would be scolded by them too. Mrs. Welch, Germaine, Sylvia, Leverette, and Ben Ben, were all part of that extended family. These people played a role in our lives and were trusted by our mother to look after us when she had to go out. From our village, we learnt compassion. We learnt how to share. We learnt politeness and mutual respect.

We learnt that with careful and dedicated planning, we could make progress in our lives, just as our parents and others had done. By gradually changing their houses from wood to concrete, or saving enough money to move, they made their lives more comfortable. With very few resources, mothers in our neighbourhood budgeted and, in many cases, raised as many as twelve to fourteen children. I give special credit to my mother for her skill at budgeting. In order to have school books, parents devised creative ways of raising funds. Times were difficult, but they found solutions to the financial challenges. I often wondered about Mrs. Hall and Mrs. Austin, who sold nuts, toffees, "ackees," sugar cakes and other goodies at the corner on Saturday mornings. Their trays always looked full, and although the items did not seem to raise much money, they were able to provide for their families through this honest labour.

Growing up in Rose Hill, a village sandwiched between two plantations – Ebworth Plantation and Alleynedale plantation - was an enriching experience. The plantation bells rang at 6:00 each morning, and labourers would pass in front of our house, heading off to the plantation with dung baskets in their hands and hoes across their shoulders, like soldiers carrying rifles. It was not uncommon for our parents to remind us that we ought to ensure that we did not end up in the "third gang" in the plantation, as these workers were referred to. This was possibly what motivated many of us to take our studies more seriously.

I still cherish images of people congregating at the stand pipe from which we all got our water. We had no running water in our house for a few years and, to get water, we had to go to the stand pipe - a public pipe - located about 30 metres from our home. I was always fascinated by how the women were able to carry water in buckets on their heads, without spilling it. We learnt how to bathe with a basin of water. Back then, we appreciated the value of that precious commodity.

Burning lamps at night and waking up early to clean the shades with newspaper was an experience which my grandson, Joel, would perhaps never understand or visualize.

Gathering on steps or street corners for bedtime stories and then running home, scared by chilling tales of "duppies" (Barbadian word for ghosts), was enough entertainment. This was before television came with shows like "Dark Shadows," which was very popular.

In the early days, there was no electricity in our village, and the lack of street lights created the perfect atmosphere for these stories. When the sugar cane plants were tall and almost ready for harvesting, our stories were about the heart man – a person who was said to cut out people's hearts and sell them to the devil.

Walking out on Sundays to visit family and friends was an important pastime, since letters took about a week to reach them and, as there were no telephones, visits were the best option.

Playing in the gully and enjoying all the seasonal fruits such as gooseberries, "dunks," tamarinds, cherries and mangoes brought intense daily pleasure. Yes, they were exciting times. We had limited resources, but no one knew, because we had a great deal of pride. By all standards, we were very poor, but we were rich in spirit and progressive in mind.

We were isolated from the city. Activities in Rose Hill and surrounding districts were enough to keep us entertained. We were unfamiliar with the word "boredom," unlike many children today, who constantly say that they are bored. We played cricket, road tennis, dominoes, football and many other children's games, including "work man."

"Work man" was a game where rocks were placed on the ground in a circular formation. If there were seven players, then there were six rocks - which we called "big rocks," to distinguish them from the pebbles. One of the players would be the "catcher" and would have no rock. That would leave six players. There was always one rock less than the number of persons remaining. The catcher would then move slightly away and the players would begin to "work." They would say "Work man" and run frenetically from rock to rock. It was important to try to get to a rock and, as there was one rock less, there was always a tense scramble. Without warning, the catcher would pounce on someone's rock and then that person who found himself or herself without a rock on which to place his feet, was "out." It was similar to musical chairs, with rocks instead of chairs and without music. There were no cassette or portable CD players in those days. Each of the players would then give a lash to the loser and, after one more rock had been withdrawn, the game would continue.

During the crop season, when sugar cane was being harvested, we had lots of activities to look forward to. We would sit by the roadside and wait to see if any canes would fall off the trucks. The more daring boys would stand at the corner of Mile and a Quarter and pull the canes off. Then we would peel them with knives or our teeth, and suck them "to our heart's delight." Our preference was for a particular brand of canes which we called "juicy canes," because they were soft and it was very easy to extract the juice.

Besides waiting for canes to fall off the trucks, we also had fun recording the license numbers of those which transported bulk sugar. We called them "bulk sugar trucks." It was exciting to see a new number. Each time we heard the sound of a truck in the distance approaching our house, we would run outside to check if it was a new number. We would then compare our listing with those of our friends to see who had the most numbers.

Another exciting activity was pitching marbles. There were two games which were very popular. One was called "Killer" and the other was "Pitching for Cowboy Pictures." "Killer" was a game where, after completing a certain process which made you a "killer," you could then "kill" any other player's marble which came near the hole by hitting it with your marble. The details of the game are a bit fuzzy in my head, but it generated a lot of interest.

The other game involved pitching for cowboy pictures. The neighbourhood shops sold bubble gum, which came with cowboy pictures. The pictures were numbered 1 to 100, and depending on how you played in any one game, you could win as many as four cowboy pictures. We spent every cent we had on bubble gum, simply to get the pictures. Quite often, we were disappointed when the picture was one which we already had, but we kept trying. Pitching for pictures was a quick way of getting more, but it was also a quick way of losing them depending on your luck or skill.

In my estimation, our most creative activity was our "sugar cane production" game in which we had our own miniature factory operation. We made small trucks comparable to the bigger trucks, complete with railings, springs, and wheels made from old tire rubber, which still bore the tracks. My best friend at primary school, Glindon Edwards, made one for me as a gift, and every day, we went to "work," pulling these trucks along the road with a piece of twine. Every so often we would stop to pick up dry cane peelings which had been thrown into the gutter, and put them on our trucks. When fully loaded, they looked exactly like the real cane trucks.

My neighbour's son had built a miniature factory. We carried the load of "cane" to his factory, where he placed them on the "scale beam." His factory looked authentic. He paid us for the cane with blue, green and red plastic toffee wrappers, which represented paper money and "coins" in the form of small, smooth-edged pieces of broken saucers or plates. We always left the factory with money in our pockets, but now I wonder how my neighbour felt about all that junk being deposited outside her home.

What imagination we had! We made our own toys, as our parents could not afford to buy them from the store. I guess that is why we appreciated our homemade toys so much.

I recall some of the card games we played when I was in my early teens. In one of those games, the loser would have to drink a large glass of water as a penalty. My aunt, the late Cora Gilkes, bought us a collection of games, which included "Snakes and Ladders," "Ludo" and other games, which she played with us although she was much older. We always remember her with fondness.

Every unoccupied area was used as a cricket pitch. Generally, my playmates included Lionel Ward, Rawle Hood and his brother Alva, Lester Small, Adrian and Tony Boyce, Jeffrey Whitney, Joseph Harvey, my cousin Halwin Skeete, and Jervis, Anthony, Winfield and Anderson Richards. The cricket games were exciting. They were often brought to an abrupt end when the owner of either the bat or ball was bowled, and refused to be out. He would end the match by putting the bat over his shoulder, or the ball in his pocket, and going home. But on the following day, we came back to play, unaffected by what had happened the day before.

We ran races and played tennis and other ball games in the road, as cars and other such vehicles passed so infrequently.

Finally and magically, television came. My grandfather, Christopher Gilkes, had been to the United States and, concluding that TV would soon come to Barbados, had returned with a television set. It sat as a curious piece of furniture in the living room of my grandparents' home for a long time. It was about a year after that that the Caribbean Broadcasting Corporation (CBC) started broadcasting television. Other people in the neighbourhood who had no TV in their own homes stood outside our grandparents' home every night and watched ours through an open window. Quite often they would become excited, making noises and cheering loudly when their favourite actors were punching each other. So, we had drama inside the living room on the television and live action outside at the window.

Initially, TV shows ran from 6:00 p.m. to 10:00 p.m. For me, this was the beginning of the end of creativity and the wider social interaction to which I referred, as the "box" took firm control of our lives. There was no more story telling. We were seeing the stories, albeit in black and white. We were now seeing the real faces of the cowboys who were in the pictures from the bubble gum packages and we were absolutely thrilled with this new experience.

Our modest lifestyle, together with the resourcefulness of our parents and the discipline imposed in our household and in the community, helped shape us. Also, the camaraderie we shared with our friends, our creativity, our spirit of exploration, and the respect we had for others, were part of a world characterized by strong communities, families and caring people.

Although we did not know it at the time, we were building a foundation which would allow us to interact confidently with people in Barbados, the region and further a field.

3

The Church

All Saints Anglican Church at which generations of my family worshipped.

The church was another central part of my upbringing. My mother insisted that we go to church with her. She sang alto in the church choir at All Saints' Church. At one time, she was also the leader of the Mothers' Union. Every Sunday morning, we walked to church for the 8:00 a.m. service. That 15-minute trek involved a steady climb along a road with a gradual incline. After church, we walked back home, as few people owned cars in those days.

My brother Steve (left) and me (age 5 years), standing in front of All Saints' Church.

We went to Sunday school at 3:00 p.m. at All Saints Girls School, where Mr. Daryll Jordan was the Sunday School Superintendent. Mr. Jordan later became the Principal of the St. Lucy Secondary School; now the Darryl Jordan Secondary School. He was a disciplinarian and a man of impeccable character.

During the Easter vacation, we attended Vacation Bible School, where I came to appreciate the Rev. Lionel Burke, the Rector at All Saints. He had the greatest impact on my life outside of the primary school setting. He was humble, very serious about his Christianity and loved working with children.

During his time as Rector, he bought a football and we all played with it at the Rectory. We recognized, from actions such as this, that he cared about the development of young people.

In 1966, he arranged for the congregation to go to the Vista Cinema to see the musical, "The Sound of Music." To children today, this might seem a small thing, but in those days, our parents had no vehicles and we only went on long journeys for church excursions. Worthing in Christ Church was therefore considered to be a very far distance from Rose Hill. Now, in many cases, families have two or more cars, and in most homes, both parents can drive, and children get driver's licenses at an early age. There is at least one television, video / CD / DVD player in every home, making it no longer necessary to go to the cinema.

I tended to use Father Burke as the model against which I assessed the actions of other priests with whom I later came into contact. His dedication and leadership style stuck in my mind as characteristics of a good leader.

As an altar server at All Saints' Church, I learnt from Mr. Collin Williams, the head of the Servers Guild at All Saints, who displayed the precision of a military leader, drilling us through sessions for servers at the altar. I found his systematic approach to ceremony fascinating. He simplified everything for us, breaking down instruction into a format which made our tasks easy to perform. I started off as a "Boat Boy," carrying a small boat-shaped brass object, which contained incense. I walked besides another server called the Thurifer, who carried a thurible in his hands. The thurible, with it long chains, was a brass container in which we would place hot coals from wood, which we burned outside the church. It was my job to place incense on the coals in the thurible using a small spoon from the container which I carried. At different stages of the service, we handed the thurible to the priest who used it at the altar.

I eventually rose to the level of Master of Ceremonies, which made me a sort of assistant for the priest in the sanctuary. I was therefore learning both responsibility and teamwork.

There were two occasions in the life of the church which were, for me, the most exciting. The first one was the Patronal Festival held during the first week in November. Different priests preached each night and members of other Anglican churches came out every night to join us. This was a very busy time for us as servers.

Our Patronal Festival always coincided with Guy Fawkes Night - a celebration which Barbadians inherited as part of our British colonial past. The use of fireworks was a big part of Guy Fawkes Night and these were readily available for purchase in our neighbourhood shops. As we walked to church, we would see little children standing at their doors, mesmerized by the starlights which glowed in their hands. In gardens in front of some homes, there were iridescent fireworks called "flower pots." Occasionally, some naughty boys would throw explosives called "bandits," which resembled large match sticks, at girls' feet and send them scampering along the road. It was an exciting time. We were awestruck by the rockets which, when ignited, shot into the air and then exploded into an array of colours.

With the advent of Barbados Independence in November, 1966, the practice of celebrating Guy Fawkes Day ended abruptly. Eventually, fireworks for private use were no longer sold in stores or village shops.

The lay reader at All Saints Church was Mr. James Irvine Griffith, the grandfather of Gay Griffith who was one of my cadets at Combermere and who had a very successful career in the band and Drums of No. 3 Company. During the Patronal Festival, I can still remember him reading a passage of scripture from Revelations 7 in a very melodious tone of voice: "And I said unto him, Sir, thou knowest. And he said to me, These are they which came out of great tribulation, and have washed their robes, and made them white in the blood of the Lamb..........."

The second special occasion was the Harvest, when we looked forward to walking up the aisle with our gifts of agricultural produce. One year, Rev. Burke formed a large youth choir with well-blended voices to sing at the Harvest. That Sunday evening, they processed up the aisle singing "For the Beauty of the Earth," using a special tune which, I think, was selected by Rev. Burke, who was an outstanding musician. The melodious tune filled the air as we eagerly awaited our turn to walk up the aisle and present our gifts.

The Sextant was Clifford Edwards, who was married to my Aunt V. He was succeeded by my cousin Marson Bend, who named his son after me. Patrick is now an organist at St. Paul's Anglican Church.

During the period of Lent, we went to church on Wednesday nights, where the focus was on the Stations of the Cross.

Church and Sunday school gave us valuable lessons for sensible living. Church life taught us the basic commandments for living, which became engrained in our lives. Later, when it became necessary to make decisions concerning moral issues, it was easy for me to choose. We had a good spiritual and ethical foundation.

4

Life at All Saints' Boys' Primary School

The old All Saints' Primary School building which is now the church hall. Inspections took place at the bottom of these steps.

My experience at All Saints' Boys Primary School was characterized by intense discipline. Punctuality was of prime importance, and on mornings, about two to five minutes before the scheduled start of school, a senior student would stand at the entrance at the top of the steps and ring the bell continuously. Anyone still approaching school would know that it was necessary to hurry. We did not have the luxury of watches, so this was a timely reminder that we had better not be late for school.

At the bottom of the steps, there would be an inspection of our hair, fingernails and general deportment. My hair was always coarse and no matter what I did, it always appeared to be uncombed. Sometimes the teacher used a steel comb or a pencil to test if it was combed properly. After I had failed this test and suffered the consequences many times, my mother devised a plan, whereby she cut a part in the middle of my hair with her scissors. After that, I had no more problems with the "hair test."

The head teacher, Mr. Charles Vaughan, and other teachers demanded accuracy in arithmetic and grammar. I had few problems with either one. My grandmother, Zulieka Gilkes, was my unofficial grammar teacher. On the many occasions that we were at her home, located on the opposite side of our street in Rose Hill, she took pains to correct our English. For example, she would say, "Not I is, I am," and correct our subject and verb agreement.

My biggest worry, however, was "mental arithmetic," classes for which were always unscheduled. Occasionally, the Headmaster would leave the platform, go to a classroom and give an impromptu mental arithmetic test. I assumed it was to see if we were concentrating. We were in an open hall, where each class could see what was happening in another class and we could see the Headmaster at his desk on the platform.

The Headmaster's intrusions were nightmares to me. Whenever he left his desk, my eyes would follow him, hoping he would not come to my class. When he did, we were so afraid that we could not even concentrate. A typical mental arithmetic question went like this:

"A lady had 20 mangoes. On the way to town she gave 6 to a friend. Further on, she got another 12 from a man. Two of these mangoes fell out of her bag. She also gave 11 to her sister…." Finally, after more twists and turns in the saga of the mangoes, he would ask the dreaded question, "How many mangoes did she have left?" Quite often, we were so scared and baffled that no one knew the answer!

I must add though, that we all had very caring teachers, including Messrs. Briggs, Timothy, Hinkson, Springer, and our Headmaster, Mr. Charles Vaughan, who played the piano. We often had gratifying sessions, singing on afternoons and sometimes marching on the platform to songs like "Toreador." I adored marching to this tune and I believe that is where my love for marching began. I developed a fascination with military marches and military bands.

Sometimes, the Headmaster awarded a prize of 25 cents to the boys who could sing the best solo. That was a lot of money in those days.

On the last day of school, the Headmaster arranged for us to have red JU-cs (a red carbonated drink) and milk as a delicious end-of-term treat. On any other day, we would have been given what was referred to as "Nutrition," which was essentially milk and biscuits.

It was a good environment for learning, and we benefitted from a solid educational foundation.

Admittedly, we were isolated from the rest of Barbados until I was about ten years old. Thus, excursions to "faraway places" such as the Crane, College Savannah, Foul Bay and King George V Park were precious. These trips took place only once a year, and visits to Bridgetown generally occurred in late August, when back to school shopping was done. If you were lucky, your mother took you to town to try on your new shoes. Most times, she would have you stand on a piece of card, draw your foot size, cut out the shape and take it to town. Sometimes she would use a slender piece of the spine of a coconut leaf to measure your foot from big toe to heel, break it at the correct length and take that to town instead. It was possible, therefore, that a child from Rose Hill might not visit Bridgetown more than once a year, or sometimes not at all.

Imagine my first day in Bridgetown after passing what was called the "Screening Test" for Combermere School at the age of ten. Everything was still relatively new for me, as I descended from the bus in Lower Broad Street and started walking towards the Fairchild Street bus terminal. My father walked next to me that morning; proud, I believe, of his son, a Combermere student! I, however, had mixed feelings. He walked me to the bus-stand to show me the way and I did not protest. I wanted to make him aware that I was big enough to take care of myself. But, after one day at school, having recognized the macho behavior of my classmates, I was determined that my father would not accompany me to the bus terminal again.

So, on reaching the drop-off point in Lower Broad Street the following morning, I noted that he was ready to take his place beside me. I said to him, "It won't be necessary this morning. I know the way." He appeared to be totally shocked, but I did not look back. I hastened along the sidewalk and went to the bus stand where I could take the Bush Hall bus to school. I wanted to stand on my own in a "big" school with many teachers and many students. I wanted to learn how to function in a new and exciting environment.

Nevertheless, I understood how my father must have felt some thirty years later, when I was taking my three daughters to a fair at their school. When they saw that I intended to enter the fairground with them, they said, "Dad, we'll be ok, you don't need to come." I smiled. They too, wanted that feeling of independence.

This feeling of independence and self-reliance is a necessary stage in our development. I think that children need to be guided, but gradually allowed to have the confidence to look after their own interests. Sometimes parents do not know how to "let go" and let their children learn how to cope with life's events.

5

The Combermere School Experience

Combermere School, affectionately called "The University of Waterford."

I was at Combermere School, loving the experience, when others thought I should have been elsewhere.

At primary school, my teachers expected a lot of me. They expected that I would be one of the students with the highest marks and would therefore be destined for Harrison College. From Class 1, I had been placed in a class above my own age level and my grades were always excellent.

When I sat the Screening Test, the forerunner to the Common Entrance exam, I was so nervous that I did not complete it properly. I knew that what I had written was accurate, but that it was not enough to pass for Harrison College. I suspect that there was huge disappointment, when it was announced that I had passed for Combermere School. The aim was to pass for Harrison College, but I had missed it. I had made third place after Harrison College and The Lodge School. Combermere was the "consolation prize," so it seemed.

My parents though, showed no visible signs of disappointment, for which I was very grateful. A group of friends sitting on a step in Rose Hill made some unkind comments about Combermere as I passed by one afternoon, "Combermere School is no school. It hardly does anything in sports." I felt awkward and embarrassed because I thought that I had displeased my teachers. However, these feelings of inadequacy were soon dispelled. There I was on that first day at Combermere, sitting in the school hall, looking around at the plaques on the wall. I noticed plaques for Barbados and Exhibition Scholarship winners, and daydreamed of having my name inscribed on one of the boards. Even then, I knew I had entered the most fascinating institution I could ever have been honoured to be part of.

At the end of the first year, we were all given an opportunity to sit the "Screening Test" again. I had placed first in class in all three academic terms and I knew I could do better, since I was more confident. However, I took the paper but chose not to answer any of the questions. I was concerned that I would have to leave Combermere and felt that the best way to prevent this was to leave both exam papers blank – Arithmetic and English, that is. I thought afterwards that the person correcting the papers must have been shocked to see that a first form student at Combermere School could not answer any of the questions! That was my first deliberate attempt to avoid the possibility of moving from Combermere.

The second such attempt to avoid leaving Combermere School occurred when I was in second form and a teacher advised my parents that I could try for a transfer to Harrison College. I was very sorry that he had raised the suggestion because it was not my intention to leave Combermere. Luckily, this plan failed. After that, I was able to comfortably enjoy my career at what we now fondly call "The University of Waterford."

Initially, I used to go directly into Bridgetown to take the Bush Hall bus on mornings. However, taking the Bush Hall bus out of Bridgetown became fraught with uncertainty, as we were never sure if we would arrive at school on time. As a result, my colleagues from St. Peter and I adopted a new plan to get to school on mornings. School began at 9.30 a.m. but we were at the bus stop at the corner of Rose Hill and Mile and a Quarter as early as 6:00 a.m. to take a bus from Boscobelle or Indian Ground. After a stop in Speightstown, the hub for buses in the north, we descended at Eagle

Hall and walked the rest of the way to school. We arrived as early as 7:30 a.m., giving us plenty of time to play before school started.

On evenings, we walked to the bus stand. We would leave school and walk through Bush Hall, Bank Hall, Queen's Park, down Broad Street, finally reaching the bus stand on the Princess Alice Highway. The last bus from Bridgetown to Speightstown departed at 6:00 p.m. After that time, one had no other choice than to hitchhike, but we did not let this stop us from being involved in extra-curricular activities.

In class, we sat in alphabetical order: Alleyne, Belgrave (Irvin), Belle (Francis), Brathwaite (Gregory), Collymore (Jeremy), Downes (Andrew), Downes (Michael)... We could scarcely remember first names, if challenged. This form, lower 1B comprised the most interesting collection of boys found anywhere - at least in my opinion. But I am sure that is how members of the other lower first forms felt. We know now, through what has become a close-knit Combermere fraternity, that we all had similar experiences.

Front row kneeling (L-R): Ervin Belgrave, Mitchie Forde, Nanton Sealy, Carlton Moore

Seated (L-R) Patrick Skeete, Harold Ruck, Charles White, Michael Waithe, Jeremy Collymore, Wayne Clarke, Michael Downes, Fernando Skeete, Beaumont Small, Holman Smith.

Back row (L-R): Jordan, Hinkson, Gregory Brathwaite, Andrew Downes, Andy Moore, Robert Smith. Michael Stuart, Hal Broomes, Ean Warner.

One of my "heroes" in class was David Stuart. He was a talented fast bowler. We were amazed that for several weeks, he was able to take so many wickets and was hardly ever struck for a boundary.

Michael Stuart and Robert Smith were our class comedians. They kept us entertained daily between classes. Robert had a brilliant mind for electronics as did Charles White. We revered them for their knowledge and skill.

Gregory Brathwaite was a scout, and we admired his dedication to the discipline.

Jeremy Collymore, Francis Belle, and Andrew Downes eventually became cadets. Jeremy is now head of the Caribbean Disaster Emergency Relief Agency (CDERA), while Francis is a high court judge of the Eastern Caribbean Supreme Court, presently assigned to St. Lucia. Andrew is a professor at the University of the West Indies.

I lost track of Michael Stuart for a while, until I saw him in the Barbados Defence Force later in the 1980s. Recently, I saw him on parade with the Barbados Legion. He too had a call to serve.

It was not difficult to settle into Combermere. Fellow students accepted you for what you were, and strong, lasting friendships developed along the way as we capitalized on canteen and lunch breaks, playing either football or cricket or pitching marbles.

I was often asked who my best friend at school was. That was always difficult for me to answer. From first to sixth form, I had many "best friends." In fact, one can argue that all the boys in the class were my best friends.

Two of those best friends who stood out were the twins, David and William Straughn, whose mother Mrs. Aida Straughn, became a second mother to me. From form upper 1B onwards, we sat together in the classroom. In order to attend parades such as Remembrance Day parade, I had to sleep over at their home. Mrs. Straughan took very good care of me.

Charles White was another best friend. He lived in Licorish Village, St. Michael and we often visited each other's homes. Much later, he and his wife Marjorie asked me to be the godfather of their daughter Alison and son Raymond.

I also spent a lot of time commuting with Jeremy Collymore, and our friendship grew to the point where we were like brothers. I also developed a strong brotherly relationship with Ean Warner, Francis Belle, Water Harper, now head of the Media Resource Centre of the Ministry of Education, Ricardo Brewster, who works in the Attorney General's office, and Eric Smith, Editor at the Nation Publishing Company, to mention just a few.

It is from these individuals that I learnt about genuine friendship. These are friends who never waiver in their support.

Envy and jealousy were unknown to us. We simply felt proud to be Combermerians. We were our brothers' keepers. We understood our school motto quite clearly: Humanitate, Religion, Industria (Humanity, Religion, Industry). Mottos are used by organizations to rally their members towards a cause or causes. Ours was very effective in making us aware of our duty of care towards our fellow man. The year 1966 in which we entered Combermere School was the year our country gained Independence and we, therefore, knew that, in our developing nation, we would also have our own roles to play later.

A number of outstanding teachers played their part in my development and by fourth form, I had made up my mind that I wanted to be a teacher. Nevertheless, in the lower and upper first forms, I pitied some of the teachers. They suffered at the hands of some students, who spent considerable time frustrating them – zeroing in on their apparent weaknesses.

For example, there was the English teacher who was always bedecked in a pin striped suit, immaculately dressed with shoes gleaming. His method of questioning was to start at the front of the class and ask questions student by student, seeming to know who among us could not provide satisfactory answers. As we rose to our feet slowly and perhaps reluctantly, he saved us the trouble by shouting "Next!" He would often shake his head from side to side in annoyance and say, "If the government wanted the benches warmed, they would put them out in the sun." In other words, he was saying that some of the students were merely "bench warmers."

On one occasion, he wanted us to give a definition of sedimentary rocks. Each student began by saying: "Sedimentary rocks are rocks which..." Then would come his response "Next," "Next," as students stared in disbelief. What he was trying to emphasize was that one could not define a word or phrase by restating part of the word(s) given. It took us a little while to understand why he responded that way. Meanwhile, he went around the class, becoming more and more frustrated.

Another teacher, a math teacher, who was somewhat advanced in age, would line up boys in front of the classroom and threaten that if another student misbehaved, he would take them all to the Deputy Headmaster. A student would then deliberately make a noise, prompting the teacher to say, "Let's go to the Deputy's office." He would proceed ahead of them to the office in a very authoritative manner. However, when he reached the Deputy's office and looked round, the boys were nowhere to be seen. They were back in the classroom, seated and laughing.

Those were very difficult days for some teachers, especially a female teacher who could not handle the students. For most of the school term, we hardly did any work in her subject area.

Those early school years were entertaining for us, but looking at it from a teacher's perspective, they must have been challenging years. The consensus was then that those were possibly the most troublesome of students who ever entered Combermere School. Having seen many students since that time, I realize that that is the typical complaint in every generation.

On the other hand, there was another English teacher who drilled us in the parts of speech. We had to analyze sentences and break them down into subject and predicate, identifying the adjectival and adverbial clauses. It was from him that we learnt the mechanics of language. For my development in that area, I thank my teacher, Captain D. Perkins who, I later discovered, was once the Officer Commanding No. 3 Company.

I also owe a debt of gratitude to my fourth form English teacher, the late Harold Wharton. He taught us the value of reading good quality novels. He taught us the B.O.A.C. of writing. In those days, BOAC (British Overseas Airways Corporation) was the name of the British airline which came to Barbados, but Mr. Wharton's acronym stood for Brief, Orderly, Accurately, and Clearly. He reminded us that we should always think of the reader and write in such a way that we were easily understood. I applied that method throughout my career, which involved writing reports; proposals; memos; minutes of meetings; and other types of documents.

Also, it was Mr. Wharton who helped me to believe that I could win a Barbados Scholarship. One day, when I was in the upper sixth form, he stopped me as I was walking along the corridor and asked me if I thought I could win a scholarship. At first I muttered, "Well.....Uhh..," then continued, "Usually, it is only students from Harrison College, Queen's College and The Lodge School who win scholarships." He asked me in a very searching manner, "What grades do you get?" I responded, "Normally,

As and Bs." Then he asked another question, "What grades do you need for a scholarship?" The words slipped out of my mouth, "As and Bs." Then a bright light went off in my head. He confirmed what I had just thought in response to his question, "So, that's all you need."

The Exhibition (Scholarship) Board displayed in the Combermere School hall.

From that moment, I changed my attitude and my approach. Mr. Wharton motivated and inspired me at a critical moment in my school career.

One night, during the summer vacation after I had completed my second attempt at French, Spanish and English, I was sitting at home when the telephone rang. My mother answered and said that it was Mr. Moore, the Headmaster. Anxiously, I took the phone from her, holding my breath as he said, "Patrick, You have won an Exhibition Scholarship!"

A thrill ran through my body. This was absolutely fantastic, especially when I considered that, on entering Combermere, I would have been below 200 on the list of performers in the Screening Test. Now I was one of the ten scholarship winners for 1975, among whom were my school mates, Jerry Thorne and David Butcher.

Jerry is now a medical doctor and David, who returned to school and won a Barbados Scholarship the following year, is now an engineer.

Mr. Deighton Maynard also played a part, in steering me towards academic success. Although I had passed my three subjects - English, French and Spanish at Cambridge Advanced level - the previous year, the grades were low. Mr. Maynard took the time to encourage me to try again. He spent over an hour outside the school's canteen convincing me that it would be beneficial to repeat sixth form. I took his advice and returned to school for an additional year.

Mr. Maynard, later Colonel Maynard, had extremely good classroom control. Everyone listened attentively to what he said. Outside of the classroom, he was involved in scouting and coaching hockey. Eventually, he took charge of the Combermere Cadet Company.

One Saturday morning, a short time before my retirement, I wanted to talk to him and I wondered where I could possibly find him. Suddenly, I remembered his dedication to Combermere School's hockey team, and I decided to go to the school at 6:30 a.m. to see if he would be there. When I arrived, he was parked in the same spot where I would have seen him every Saturday for over forty years, reading the newspaper as he waited for students to arrive for hockey practice. His commitment knew no equal.

In the sixth form, I met Mr. Carl Wade, now Dr. Wade, for the first time. His English literature classes were eagerly anticipated. I admired the way he analyzed the literature, and it was easy to follow him as he discussed themes, characters, and technique and taught us to exhaust the topics.

One day, he invited me to come out of the classroom into the corridor and explained that my essays, though grammatically correct, were too short. He advised me to exhaust the topic by looking at it from many different angles. I listened carefully and improved significantly. Much later, during my first week at the St. Augustine Campus of the University of the West Indies in Trinidad, one of the lecturers in Spanish literature, Dr. Kim Lawrence, challenged me to prepare a book review on a novel called "El Negro Francisco." She had asked us to state our names for her benefit and, as I spoke, she noticed my Barbadian accent. I was the only Barbadian in the group, and she singled me out to do the first book review, giving me one week to complete it. Armed with the techniques drilled into us by Mr. Wade, I completed the task quite easily and presented the review to the class. After the session, some Trinidadian classmates asked me, "Who taught you to do book reviews like that?" I said, "I had an excellent English literature teacher named Mr. Carl Wade."

Mrs. Dorien Pile taught me human and economic geography. Her classes were always very interesting, and she was well respected by the students.

What I will always remember about her though, is the support she gave me after I had realized my dream of becoming a teacher and was experiencing one of my lowest moments. At the time, she was Deputy Principal, and I had gone to the school during the vacation to find out about the Spanish exam results, as I had taught Spanish to fifth formers. I was disappointed - devastated when I saw that my students had not performed well. I

Mrs. Dorien Pile (second from right) among her cadets at the St. Lucy Depot of the BDF.

questioned whether I was making a difference and was on the verge of giving up. Mrs. Pile intervened and reminded me of the effort I had put in. She advised that, if possible, I should find a little time after school to give a few classes. I took her advice and sought parents' permission to conduct classes for one hour after school. The parents were shocked that there was no fee. At the end of the process, all twenty-five students passed the Spanish exam. There were fifteen distinctions and ten passes.

Mrs. Pile's advice boosted my career significantly. Thereafter, I think students felt that if they joined my class, they had a reasonable chance of passing their Spanish exams. I also started teaching advanced level Spanish to sixth form students and earned a record of 100% passes.

I felt that every student in my class ought to be given a reasonable chance of passing the exam, and I used a range of methods to achieve this objective. One day, I met a member of the school's board in a social setting and she complimented me on the work I was doing with the students. She said I was doing "a wonderful job."

I wanted Spanish to come alive for my students and for them to have an enthralling experience in my classes. In 1986, I took twenty-five students to Venezuela at Christmas time to expose them to the spoken language and culture of Spanish-speaking people. Five other teachers accompanied the group. We raised the funds needed to make the trip, which was an unforgettable experience. We visited the German Village, known as Colonia Tovar, and travelled up the mountains in a cable car. We witnessed many activities in Caracas, the capital, and the students were able to use their language in stores, at restaurants, on the streets and in the hotel.

I also remember Mrs. Pile's husband, Mr. Colvin Pile, who had been my favorite French teacher. He was a very good teacher and I was highly motivated. I wanted to do my best for him, and he rewarded me with a large LaRousse French dictionary, which I used throughout my career as a student of French. I now have a better understanding of the type of personal sacrifice teachers like him would have made to keep us motivated.

We learnt Latin in upper first and second forms. We were told that it was a dead language, but we enjoyed it, especially as it was taught by Messrs. Arthur Sealy and Keith King. We took great pleasure from quoting Latin questions such as "Ubi festinas? (Where are you hastening to?) and making statements such as "Agricola terram arat." (The farmer ploughs the land). From words like "vulnero," which means in English "I wound," linked to the word "vulnerability," we began to decipher the meaning of many English words. Latin, though considered a "dead" language, came alive in our grasp of English words and expressions.

Mr. Charlie Pilgrim was, in my estimation, an excellent history teacher and an outstanding principal. His history classes came alive through his dramatizations in which vocal variety and tone always created excitement and laughter. When I had become a teacher and he was Principal, I felt comfortable knowing that he would treat me fairly and listen to my point of view.

Mr. Harry Sealy, who was in charge of the junior school, came to our form from time to time, as a substitute teacher, with whom the boys instantly built a rapport. It was people like him who made me realize that the question of class control and discipline was somehow wrapped up in how the teacher approached the students. These were valuable career lessons for me.

Teachers, whom I classified as excellent, showed an interest in students both inside and outside the classroom. It is noteworthy that the three most significant sets of advice which I got were passed on to me outside the classroom in a face-to-face encounter with a caring teacher and not during a formal classroom session. It was Mr. Maynard spending one and a half hours outside the canteen encouraging me to return to school an additional year in the sixth form, Mr. Wharton stopping me on the corridor to ask about the scholarship and Mr. Carl Wade calling me out into the corridor and coaching me on how to write better essays that made a substantial difference in my life.

Hence, the individuals I mentioned, personified the qualities I thought would be needed to be a successful teacher. They all had contrasting styles, but what was common was their love for children and their desire to make the teaching/learning process pleasurable and worthwhile.

The Combermere School old scholars made a strong impression on me. They came into the school every day during Combermere Old Scholars' Week, which was held in October every year. They spent each morning at Assembly reassuring us about the value of the experience at Combermere. Even now, some people refer to it as indoctrination, but it helped to keep us focused.

I spent many hours at Combermere on weekends, and was amazed at how often old scholars holidaying in Barbados or attending family funerals would enter the school grounds and walk around. They would often show their families their old classrooms and try to identify the desks at which they sat. Even if they had only two days available to them, some portion of that time had to be spent reminiscing on the compound of Combermere School.

This strong sense of belonging to an institution goes far back into the past. In my book "The Combermere Cadet", I wrote about a Combermerian named Joseph Chamberlain Hope, who served in World War 1, in 1916. He was stationed in Palestine and despite being engaged in the war effort, he still found time to write to his former Headmaster at Combermere to inquire about the school's performance in exams and whether Combermere had selected a school song. The officer responsible for screening letters wrote at the bottom of the letter that he was sorry to intrude, but he was compelled to say that J.C. Hope was a credit to his school. I am sure that he too marveled at this dedication to the old school shown by Private Hope.

I understood this feeling of belonging. Combermere School had become my home away from home.

The most captivating aspect of my school life was my involvement in No.3 Company, Barbados Cadet Corps. I had stayed on the sidelines for a few years and watched the cadets parading, never thinking I could live up to what was required. This is usually what happens when we stay outside and look in.

One day, a teacher, Mr. Jeff Sealy, who had been a cadet and who had just left school, spent an entire lesson talking to us about the importance of joining the Cadet Corps. By the following week, I was a recruit. It was the best decision I ever made!

Company Sergeant Major Kenneth Harvey.

What was intriguing to me was that in the No. 3 Company there were schoolboys who could easily be mistaken for adult teachers. People like Charlie Belle, Ken Harvey, the Sergeant Major who trained me as a recruit, Roger Thorpe, Trevor Browne, and James Bradshaw stood tall as role models and displayed a maturity which belied their ages. This was the essence of cadet training. A schoolboy was suddenly thrown into an adult role and given responsibility similar to that of a teacher.

The rank structure and the stripes held a special attraction for us as recruits.

I was particularly impressed by another senior cadet. He was Head Boy, Cadet Under Officer and had also won a Barbados Scholarship. That individual was Mr. Trevor Shepherd, now a medical doctor. I had noted how scholars at Combermere were also fully involved in cadets, cricket, hockey, football, athletics and many other activities. I knew that I would not be compromising my school work.

Although he did not know it, Trevor Shepherd was my mentor. I had so far placed first in class at the end of every school term, and I did not want my parents to complain about my involvement in cadets. I therefore developed a strategy for keeping abreast with school work.

Recruiting was exciting, having to learn the various drill movements and respond to orders such as "Left turn," "Stand at Ease," "'Shun," "About Turn" and many more.

Finally, we passed the recruit test and were eligible to wear a uniform. I received a blue beret, a khaki shirt, a pair of short khaki pants, khaki coloured puttees, blue hose top socks, web belts and leather soled boots, reminiscent of those worn by British soldiers in World War II. We had to be careful when running on concrete surfaces in those boots, as it was easy to slide and fall. As a young boy, walking to the bus stop on mornings, I often sensed people in the neighbourhood looking at me with some curiosity. They were not accustomed to seeing this type of uniform.

Since the Cadet Corps had only been formed in three schools, the uniform attracted much attention, and we wore it proudly every Friday for school parade. We worked hard to get the brasses on our belts shining and our boots gleaming. We learnt quickly how to do a "water shine." Using polish, cotton wool and water, we rubbed the tips of the boots gently in a circular motion until they shone brighter and brighter.

That Summer vacation when we had not been informed about cadet camp, and were unsure of the dates, I had heard a notice on the radio about an International Cadet Camp and decided to attend. When I reached St. Ann's Fort, I saw my friend Jeremy Collymore, who was one of my classmates. It soon dawned on us that we were at the wrong camp, and should have attended the Basic Training Camp which had preceded this one. Would we be accepted in camp? Would we be sent home? Would we miss out on exams? And if so, how would it affect our progress in the cadet company?

These were the burning questions we asked ourselves.

6

My First Camp Experience

Being in the wrong camp gave me an uncomfortable feeling. It felt as though we were being watched and everyone was thinking about the nicest way to tell us that we had to pack our kit and go home. Jeremy and I thought that the best way to handle the situation was to get on with the activities and behave as though we had a right to be there. The misunderstanding was not totally our fault. Those were the days before it was mandatory to send letters to parents seeking their permission for their children to participate in camps.

It was a 3-week international camp at which Part 2 Army Proficiency Course (APC) training was being conducted.

We trained from Monday to Friday, and were given each weekend free. We could either go home on weekends and return on Sunday night or stay in camp and spend time going to the beach or the cinema. Those were the days when Canadian Armed Forces aircrafts brought cadets from Canada and the Caribbean to Barbados. Jamaica, Trinidad and Guyana were also camp destinations operating simultaneously.

It was a very interesting process. A plane from Canada transported Canadian cadets to Jamaica, Barbados, Trinidad and Guyana. Cadets from St. Vincent and St. Lucia gathered in Barbados to board this plane. At the end of the camp the plane departed from Guyana and collected the cadets in reverse order. In this arrangement, Combermere was given sixteen places. Usually, six cadets from Combermere went to Canada, four to Jamaica, four to Trinidad and two to Guyana. The trip to Canada was obviously the most popular.

I wondered whether I would ever have the opportunity to attend one of those international camps overseas.

Meanwhile, in 1971 when some of our colleagues were camping in other countries, we were at St. Ann's Fort enjoying the international camp. Combermere shared a barrack room with the Jamaicans and I developed friendships with them. The cadets in that barrack room were all in the same platoon.

At the young age of fifteen, I was therefore exposed to people from Canada and the wider Caribbean. As fascinated as I was by their different cultures and accents, I felt the bond which united us in one activity – "cadetting." Jeremy and I were allowed to do the APC exam, despite protests from a few senior cadets who felt that we should do Basic Test (BT) first. Fortunately, Lieutenant Colonel Leonard Banfield, who kept a close eye on cadet activities allowed us to stay.

Colonel Banfield was a man of contrasts. He made cadets shiver in their boots as he walked majestically and menacingly down the line inspecting the platoons. We thought he had an aversion to long hair, having sent so many cadets off the parade ground because of their hair. There was even a time when he made cadets going overseas have haircuts just before boarding a flight to Canada.

He was stern, focused on discipline and required that we be neat and well groomed. But he was a fair, humble man who loved children. Jeremy and I were once sent to the butts to patch targets on the large shooting range at Paragon. This task was designed to economize on targets and cadets were stationed in the butts to lower the targets and patch them. This duty would be rotated so that everyone would have an opportunity to shoot. We had the pleasure one day of sitting in the butts with Col. Banfield helping to patch targets and telling jokes. We were surprised that a Commanding Officer of the Barbados Regiment could "come down to our own level." This impression of what a leader could be has stayed with me throughout my career.

We learnt a lot at this International Camp and, on returning to school in the 1971-72 term, we were prepared to do our best.

Lt Col Leonard Banfield sitting on the floor in the front center among cadets. Behind him are some of the Barbados Regiment personnel who conducted training in camp.

7

A New Beginning

Lt. HD Maynard

Our geography teacher, with whom we associated scouting and hockey, marched on to the square to take command as our new Officer Commanding. He was then Second Lieutenant Deighton Maynard. His words still echo in my ears, "I would rather have a small, efficient company than a large ragged squad."

This was the start of something special, which transformed Combermere School for more than a decade. Lt. Maynard brought an exciting programme, demanded high standards and kept us looking forward to more and more exhilarating activities. Mock battles, route marches, weekend hiking activities (bivouacking), ceremonial parades at Independence time and Speech Day, and overseas camps were all part of an ingenious plan to keep us fully occupied. Instead of remaining a small company, the ranks of No. 3 Company expanded rapidly.

Students tend to gravitate towards teachers who care and Lieutenant Maynard did care. He spent long hours outside the staff room chatting with students.

1972: Hike to Mt. Misery. Author is fourth from left.

Guard Mounting at Oxnard 1971: Cpl. Yard, Francis Belle, David Straughan, Andy Williams, Kempton Nurse, Yearwood, Trevor Headley, Jeremy Collymore and the author.

Within five to six years, No. 3 Company had 3 infantry platoons, a band and approximately 120 cadets in the unit.

Early in his tenure, the then Second Lieutenant Maynard conducted an NCO course at Oxnards, St. James, near the old sugar cane mill. It was a few months prior to a scout jamboree, and during that camp, we helped to plant grass seeds. I remember Major McConney visiting and talking to us briefly about the possibility of establishing a Regular Army. This training camp was, for me, my first real exposure to leadership training. It was a very impactful experience.

Returning to school, we set our sights higher and started putting what we had learnt into practice.

June of 1972 was a special month for me. One day, I was in the school canteen looking at the Weekly Orders which had just been posted on the notice board which bore the Combermere Cadet Crest. By Wednesday or Thursday of each week, we consulted this board for details of training or any other notices. It was very strategically placed to ensure that information was readily available.

I was overjoyed when I saw my name on the list of cadets selected to travel overseas, as part of the Canadian Caribbean Exchange. This was going to be a very special experience, given that very few of us could afford to travel to these countries with our families.

I could not wait to get home and tell my family about this opportunity. But by the afternoon, something had occurred at school to dampen my excitement.

8

My First Overseas International Camp

According to the listing on the notice board, I was the sole Combermerian selected for camp in Guyana, while four of my colleagues were selected for Trinidad. I was pleased to be among those sixteen cadets selected to travel overseas. However, I did not understand, then, how arduous the Guyana leg was considered to be by those who had either participated in or heard stories about the training.

After each exchange camp, cadets would tell stories about their experiences to motivate others who were awaiting selection. Their tales were a very strong incentive.

On the day I discovered I had been selected to go to Guyana, I was sitting contentedly in class, fantasizing about camping overseas, when a group of about four senior cadets came to my classroom and approached my desk. They told me how difficult the Guyana training would be and that I should reject the offer because it would be too hard for me. They noted that another senior cadet, who was much bigger and more muscular than me, attended that camp and was frazzled when he returned to Barbados.

I understood that it was done out of concern for me, but I was "down-spirited" afterwards.

Author waiting to board the Canadian Armed Forces aircraft at Seawell Airport, 1972.

However, on returning home that evening, I told my mother what had happened. She had a very simple, intuitive response to me. She said, "Mr. Maynard selected you. He must have seen something in you. I trust his judgment. Do not let anyone deter you!" And so, with an open mind, I accepted the assignment and prepared myself for what I expected was going to be a challenging experience. When the big day came, we headed to the airport. I had travelled before with my sister and brother to Martinique in 1971, but this was the first time I would be travelling alone and would be away from home for three long weeks. The camp was scheduled from July 22 to August 14, 1972.

The airport was a hive of activity, with cadets from Barbados, en route to training camps in Trinidad and Guyana. Cadets from St. Vincent and St. Lucia, who had stayed overnight in Barbados, were also gathered for departure via a Canadian Armed Forces aircraft.

I said goodbye to my parents, feeling very proud to be able to go off on my own - to be able to take care of myself.

Finally, we were in the air, flying to Trinidad, our first stop. When we disembarked, we were transported to Mausica Teachers' Training College, to overnight, before proceeding by the same aircraft to Guyana the next morning. We were thrilled to be spending a night in another Caribbean country. The next morning, we were off to Guyana.

Travelling over Guyana was a lesson in geography. Mrs. Pile, Mrs. Jebodsingh and Lieutenant Maynard had all taught us physical and economic geography, and here I was trying to apply my learning.

It was a very long trip, and from the air we could see large rivers, trees and great expanses of land. The view was breathtaking!

Three instructors from the GDF in the foreground.

On arrival at the airport in Guyana, we were greeted by soldiers from the Guyana Defence Force. I understood, as time passed, how closely we were all related. There were many Guyanese with Barbadian grandfathers, grandmothers, parents, uncles, aunts, and other relatives. This made us feel very much at home.

About two years before I retired, I was in the Barbados Defence Force Officers' Mess and a former Guyana Defence Force (GDF) soldier, whose surname was also Skeete, sought me out, having heard that I was an officer in the Barbados Defence Force. Although many years had passed since we had last seen each other, there was still a bond – a special camaraderie shaped by those three weeks in his country.

The Camp Commandant, Captain Mitchell, from the GDF and his team, including Warrant Officer 1 Vancouten; Lieutenant Boyce; Corporals Patterson and Raymond; and other instructors were outstanding trainers, who delivered instruction in orienteering; skill at arms; field craft; jungle craft; physical training and much more.

The jungle was fascinating and orienteering in that environment, where every tree we passed looked like the one before, was challenging. Overhead, the leaves interlocked to provide a canopy, blocking out any light at night time. There were also sections of the path where the consistency of the soil was much like quicksand into which our feet would sink. We therefore learnt to walk along the edges of the path close to the roots of the trees. And yes, there were our "friends," the snakes, which we dreaded. We reminded the soldiers that in Barbados, the most frightening creatures were centipedes and vicious dogs, and that we were mortally afraid of snakes. We did see a few of them, but the soldiers guided us past them.

Jungle craft showed how skillfully the Guyanese soldiers could hide and blend with the jungle environment, either in trees or under the ground. What a spellbinding experience it was to see them in action.

One particular exercise kept us in the jungle until nightfall, when it was totally dark. We could not see our hands. We could see nothing but the snakes crawling all over us in our vivid imaginations. It was a chilling experience, but we learnt to depend on the skills we had been taught. Fortunately, it was only for one night.

During those three weeks, we completed a full drill course and a weapons course from small arms to the general purpose machine gun. Sergeant Major Vancouten and Cpl. Patterson, who were our main drill instructors, often stopped and referred us to the drill pamphlet, to remind us that it was all standard, current military practice.

My level of physical fitness sky-rocketed. Our physical training began with a morning run, the length of which increased every day during the first week.

By the second week, rifles were added; as we did Battle PT. In addition to running long distances, we now had to contend with the weight of a rifle. It also meant that each morning we had to wake up at 4:00 and run five-hundred meters to the armoury to secure our weapons and then run back to the barracks. This was before we had even started physical training for the day.

I was not prepared to fail, and I succeeded in completing all the activities. I also needed to prove to senior cadets at home that you could not judge someone by his physical appearance. I was quite slim, but I was determined and I knew that Lieutenant Maynard expected much of me.

Captain Mithchell (GDF), Camp Commandant, sitting on the beach among cadets.

I have always been impressed when great leaders are able to "come down to the level of the cadets." I saw another example of this in Captain Mitchell. One day we were taken to the beach and I was quite surprised that he just sat there casually among us. Normally, we feared him because of his tough stance and the way he glared at us during inspections. However, he showed us a different side on the beach. It was a reminder of what Lt. Maynard, or Col. Banfield would have done back at home.

Familiar persons attending this camp were Adult Warrant Officer Zeno Crepin, who became Commandant of the Trinidad and Tobago Cadet Force; Company Quarter Master Yearwood of St Vincent, who became Regimental Sergeant Major; and Sergeant Vernon Gittens, now my fellow officer in the BDF.

Vernon and I were both made Officer Cadets of the Barbados Regiment in 1975. There were only four Barbadians in that Guyana camp: namely, Sergeant Senhouse and Corporal Rollins from The Lodge School and Sergeant Dowell from Harrison College. The Guyana camp was obviously not the most sought after camp, perhaps because it involved very tough training. In all, four cadets went to Guyana; eighteen went to Canada and ten to Trinidad. For me, Guyana was the best choice ever, and on my return, I was feeling "on top of the world", confident that I had a lot to offer No. 3 Company.

I still cherish memories of that campsite at Timehri, home of the Training Corps of the GDF.

(Photo at left): Entire group at camp. Commandant Capt. Mitchell, Guyana Defence Force (seated 8th from left). Sergeant Vernon Gittens, Barbados Regiment (seated 4th from left) and Contingent Commander. Sergeant Major Vancouten (7th from right).

9

A Family Called to Service

Jennifer Haynes

Patricia Carrington

While I was following my dreams, my siblings were also following theirs, focusing on service to others.

My sister Jennifer was attracted to the nursing profession. She entered the Tercentenary School of Nursing, and shortly after graduating, she travelled to the United Kingdom to study midwifery and pediatric nursing. This journey gave her the opportunity to serve as a nurse in the United Kingdom, the Bahamas and Florida. Married to Wendell Haynes, and retired from 2010, she spends her time as a volunteer in the Episcopal Church community.

My other sister Patricia was keen on teaching. She was trained at Erdiston Teachers Training College in the days when students lived in residence for a period of time. She also completed the Certificate in Educational Management and Administration at the School of Education, University of the West Indies. She became a primary school teacher and ended her career as Senior Teacher.

As a teenager, she was involved in voluntary services. She served as Sunday School Superintendent and teacher at All Saints Anglican Church, and managed the All Saints Church Girl Guide Company for many years. She and my mother were members of the Evangelical Singers, a group from St. Peter, whose members enjoyed moving around the island on Sunday evenings visiting shut-ins and children's homes to bring cheer to the residents.

Stevenson Skeete

Patricia and her husband, John Carrington, have three children: Kevin, Kay and Kris.

My brother Stevenson also experienced life as a cadet. He joined the unit at Harrison College, and reached the rank of Cadet Under Officer. We attended a camp in St. Lucia together. We also played guitar in a Barbadian band in Canada Hall of the St. Augustine Campus of the University of the West Indies, Trinidad.

Steve's passion is agriculture. He won the John R. Bovell Scholarship, which allowed him to pursue studies at the St. Augustine Campus. He then spent his entire career in the Ministry of Agriculture as an agronomist. He received a national award for "Excellence in Research" from the Ministry of Agriculture and an award from the Food and Agricultural Organization (FAO) for his contribution to agriculture. In 1990, he successfully completed his master's degree in tropical horticulture and crop science at the University of London, United Kingdom. He worked closely with farmers over the years, helping them overcome the challenges of tropical crop production.

Steve as a cadet

Steve and his wife, Junetta, have two children: Gregory and Jeniece.

Frederick Cadogan, my other brother, was an outstanding chef, serving Barbados through the hotel and tourism industry before he retired. His daughter's name is Sheena.

10

Innovative Thinking

Drum Corps, 1970.

The development of No. 3 Company (Combermere Cadet Company) accelerated steadily under the astute leadership of Lt. Deighton Maynard.

Every year, from 1972 to 1979, there was something new and sensational to look forward to in the company. Such was the creative leadership of Lieutenant Maynard.

In 1973, he noted that a band would enhance the unit. There was already a thriving drum corps, providing excellent music for our annual route march to sugar cane factories. Sugar Cane factories offered us the opportunity to enjoy cane juice.These drummers and buglers played a variety of melodies which surpassed the songs normally associated with the bugle, and made long marches easier to bear. Bass drummers, the late Corporal Parris (Babsy) and Corporal Kennedy, and buglers, Corporal Francis Belle, Lance Corporals Burke, Charlie Pile, Trevor Headley, Delbert White, and

L.Cpl. Trevor Hunte, L.Cpl. Trevor Headley, L.Cpl. Charlie Pile, L.Cpl. Delbert White.

many others before them, were simply outstanding.

But Lieutenant Maynard was a man of vision. He engaged the music form at school and drafted the first set of band members into the Cadet Corps.

I was on the parade square that afternoon when they "fell in" to be recruits. I could not help but think that it was an experiment which only Lieutenant Maynard could attempt. It was based on their strong acceptance of him as a caring teacher. Leadership is about the ability to influence people to achieve a common goal or goals. One of the cadets, Adrian Johnson, who was drafted into the band and went on to have a very successful career in No. 3 Company, expressed his feelings in very graphic details in a facebook comment which he shared with me and authorized me to quote in this book:

> Our first lessons were not like I expected, in fact for weeks I never saw an instrument. Instead, we were taken onto the school's car park, which doubled as the parade square. Basic Training involved learning to march, falling in, forming a single line based on height, two lines based on numbers and eventually three lines. The commands still ring out in my head, just like I expected. There was some excitement performing these Magical Steps and it felt encouraging... I was drafted into the cadets when the No.3 Company was hoping to create a more complete band. The band went on to play full instrumentation seated and marching. We appeared on television, at Illaro Court, Government House and many special locations throughout the island. We played on invitation at NIFCA and tore the house down with our popular Hootenanny melody. We started Tin Pan Alley, the birth child of Terry Ally and hard work of Jeffrey Bostic, the then Drum Major. Christopher Atherley was our flamboyant conductor, on loan from the Police Band. He molded us into young maestros.

The Combermere School Cadet Band was a big hit on the island and was well respected for its ability.

This testimony speaks volumes about what the No.3 Company meant for cadets.

Finale of Tin Pan Alley 1979. No 3. Company Band and Drums shine under the baton of Superintendent Gordon Lovell in front of a packed audience.

Author accompanying Cdt. David Batson and Cdt. Cassius Shepherd at Tin Pan Alley 1979

The Combermere Cadet Band, as it was known, became a household name in Barbados during those years. It was called on for national events such as the Independence Day Parade and the Holetown and Oistins Fish Festivals. The band performed for important BDF activities and entertained congregations at churches all around Barbados, and youthful audiences at primary and secondary schools.

The close association with the Royal Barbados Police Force was very helpful to the band, which benefited from their music scores and expert training.

Band and Drums of No. 3 Company in the early 1980s outside the BDF Officers' Mess.

Many outstanding musicians on the local music scene came out of the cadet band. Indeed, local festivals such as Crop Over, still benefit from the talent of these people who play in various bands, and provide music for the calypsonians.

By 1995, when the Barbados Cadet Corps was seeking to form a National Band to involve other schools, the Combermere Cadet Band had been performing since 1973 - a period of twenty-three years. By this time, the new National Cadet Band still had a strong nucleus of Combermerians and this lent to its immediate success. With the development of the band, we continued to marvel at the innovative spirit of Lt. Maynard.

11

Introduction of Females

Female cadets fully integrated into No. 3 Company, 1975.

The creation of the band and drums section was one of three significant developments in the Corps which originated at Combermere. The second was the unprecedented enrollment of females into the cadet company. The third was the recommencement of overseas camps.

In September 1973, five girls who were my classmates, and who had transferred from Christ Church Foundation School to join the sixth form at Combermere, created history when they were admitted to the No. 3 Cadet Company.

It was the first time in the history of the Cadet Corps in Barbados that females had joined the Corps or, indeed, the military.

I was standing with Lieutenant Maynard, chatting in the area outside the No. 3 Company office when five girls approached him to ask if they could join the Cadet Corps. Although we had been accustomed to having boys only, their request did not surprise me. Combermere had started accepting girls into the sixth form and these young ladies were very much involved in the life of the school. Margot Greene, Rozanne Jones, Marlene Sivers, Mary Redman and Angela Aimey were the five girls.

Realizing how serious they were, Lt. Maynard, said that he would discuss the matter with Col. Banfield, Commanding Officer of the Barbados Regiment. The rest is now history. Permission was granted.

By 1976, Combermere had started to accept female students into school at first form level. This meant that the girls could now recruit at an earlier age.

Decisions often necessitate adjustments. When one sees female students at either Combermere School, in the No. 3 Company or in the entire Corps, it seems natural that they should be routinely participating in activities and be fully integrated. However, in 1975, we grappled with the question of how best to incorporate them into our school structure.

When girls first joined classes in the sixth form, school authorities were required to provide washroom facilities and other female amenities. Moreover, the chorus of the school song was changed from "Up Boys, Truest Fame lies in high endeavor" to "Up then, truest fame lies in high endeavor" and the Combermere Old Boys' Association became the Combermere Old Scholars' Association. As Officer Commanding No.3 Company, I had to consider separate arrangements for bathrooms and other facilities when organizing camps, and plan carefully for the integration of the females into cadet training exercises. Parents were concerned about their daughters' safety and it became necessary to have adult female supervision. There were no female officers in those days, but with senior girls in the sixth form, it was easier to handle these challenges. Also, from time to time female soldiers from the Barbados Regiment helped to supervise the girls.

Margaret Sivers and Beverley Smith (now Hinkson), were some of these mature females who came after the first set of female cadets. They made it easier for girls like Maylene Sargeant and Sharon Mahon, who were among the first group of females to join the No. 3 Company in the lower school.

The success of any experiment depends largely on the effort of the people involved and those who stand to benefit from the experience. Having made the bold move to gain approval and join the Corps, the first cadre of females proved that they could stand proudly in the ranks beside their male colleagues. They set a high standard, expected no special treatment and endured the same training conditions as the boys.

The disadvantage of girls joining in the sixth form was that their exposure was brief and they did not have enough time to move through the ranks. The only person to receive a rank among this first set of girls in the sixth form was Margot Greene, who became a Lance Corporal.

Author with Major Margot Greene, QC.

After leaving school, Margot returned to the Corps to render service and was appointed Major. She continues to be a dear friend of mine. When she became a Queen's Counsel I was invited to the ceremony, and was very honoured to attend. This is another strong friendship built in the Cadet Company at Combermere School.

There is no doubt that Lt. Maynard transformed the Combermere Cadet Company and, in a sense, transformed Combermere School. When I was a young officer in the Barbados Regiment, I was once advised by a senior officer that the key to success was to look and learn from senior officers. I learnt from the very best – Lieutenant Maynard.

12

Personal Achievements

Receiving my prizes from the Governor-General, Sir Arleigh Winston Scott GCMG, GCVO Speech Day 1973

One of the greatest moments in my academic career was when I received the Armstrong Memorial Prize for best performance in the Cambridge Ordinary Level examinations during Combermere School's Speech Day Ceremony in 1973. I had the honour of receiving these from the then Governor-General, Sir Arleigh Winston Scott GCMG, GCVO.

I had previously been awarded the Kinch and Carter Scholarships. The Kinch Scholarship was a monetary prize of BD$100. With these funds, I bought my first tape recorder to record the language exercises. I also used it as one of the tools for reviewing my various subjects. This was the first item of such value that I had ever possessed. Our financial circumstances would not have permitted me to own such a device, so the tape recorder was a special gift to myself.

The Carter Scholarship was also a monetary award. I received BD$300, with which I bought an airline ticket to Martinique and covered a large part of the fare for my sister Patricia and my brother Steve, who accompanied me. We stayed with Mr. Rene Rocher and his wife Gilbert, in Fort de France. They had two sons Romule and Miguel and a daughter Brigette. During that visit, we also spent time in Vauclin at the home of Mrs. Rocher's sister and family – the Lostaus. Their daughters Lilas, Josiane and Emilie and sons Gilles and Eric became very dear friends of ours.

Needless to say, this seventeen-day visit to Martinique boosted my appreciation for and use of French.

This had been my first overseas trip, made possible through hard work and the Carter Scholarship. In my last year at school (1975), I was school Captain, won an Exhibition Scholarship in modern languages, and earned the rank of Cadet Senior Under Officer. I no longer had to wonder whether my name would ever appear on the awards board. The dream had become reality!

In that same year, also, I had the honour of being the most senior cadet from among the three existing school companies attending the summer camp in St. Vincent.

Prospect House, 1975. Front row: Sgt Neil Haynes, CUO Francis Belle, Author, CUO Benjie Cummins, Sgt Farnum

Rear rank: CSM Ian Brathwaite (extreme left), CQMS Clyde Parris (secnd from left), CSM Keith Squires (extreme right)

At University of the West Indies in Trinidad, I graduated with Second Class Honours in modern languages and won the French Embassy Prize for outstanding performance in French in 1977 and 1979.

While teaching at Combermere, I successfully completed the Diploma in Education at the University of The West Indies, gaining a distinction in both the theory and practice of education which, I understand, was a special achievement. This prepared me for my role of designing and implementing training courses for adults and children later in my career at the Barbados Cadet Corps Headquarters.

It was often necessary to remind people who had done instructor's courses in the military, that I was a trained teacher. I understood how children learned and knew how to use the methods most appropriate for cadets. I had simply adjusted my approach to suit the requirements of the military setting. The fundamentals of the teaching/learning process remained the same.

13

Initiation into Adult Leadership

Having successfully completed my studies at Combermere, I turned my attention to my University Career. News of the Exhibition Scholarship set me thinking about my options. I had not applied to universities overseas and I did not want to give up the opportunity to study in another Caribbean country. I requested that the Ministry of Education defer the scholarship for one year to give me time to make the necessary applications. Approval was granted.

I had given no thought to being an adult officer in the Cadet Corps. Since I was not a teacher at Combermere, I felt that I could only serve when I had completed my degree and had possibly gained a place on the teaching staff at Combermere.

Lt. Maynard was thinking ahead of me, because, on my last day at school, as I handed him my cadet uniform at the door of the staff room, he surprised me by saying, "I have plans for you."

Within a month, I was in Colonel Banfield's office signing up to be a member of the Barbados Regiment. I was soon to be Officer Cadet Skeete, in the company of other outstanding leaders such as Officer Cadets Florence Gittens, Randolph Straughn, Vernon Gittens and Joel Ward.

During the period 1975-76, I was also fortunate to be teaching French and Spanish at Ellerslie Secondary School. I enjoyed the assignment and was glad that Mr. Cuthbert Brathwaite, the Headmaster and, coincidentally, the father of my Cadet Corps and BDF colleague, Major Charles Brathwaite, was interested in having students from Ellerslie School join the Cadet Corps. Sergeant Presteen Sobers of the Barbados Regiment was on staff at the time, and although there was a strong possibility that a unit would have been started, it did not get going until 1978. Meanwhile, I continued to assist Lieutenant Maynard at Combermere, travelling by bus to Eagle Hall on Friday evenings and then walking from there to Combermere to help with routine training.

I spent only one year at Ellerslie, but I learnt a lot about teaching and met wonderful young people, many of whom are still my friends today. I cultivated strong friendships with teachers such as Mrs. Doriel Hazzard, the Year Head for my third form students, and developed a great deal of respect for Mr. Brathwaite, who was an astute administrator. He demanded high standards from teachers, and to ensure that we met those standards, he would visit the classes to see what was going on and how we were conducting ourselves. We were always conscious that he could appear any time, and we had to make sure that we were managing our classes properly. This helped me tremendously as I embarked on a teaching career after completing my university studies.

My first day as a teacher is still very fresh in my mind. I was assigned to Form 3A1, and among the students in that class were Hyacinth Thompson, Andrea Williams, Leila Hack, Margaret Johnson, Augustina Hinds, Gabrielle Clarke, Trevor Roberts (who later became my brother-in-law), and Heth Padmore. They had been accustomed to having female French and Spanish teachers, and the arrival of a male teacher was viewed with skepticism. I was substituting for Mrs. Celeste Porte, who was on leave for one year. She had set a very high standard as their teacher, and I was required to fill a pair of very large boots. When I entered the classroom, I heard a collective sigh from the students, and Hyacinth and Andrea who sat near the door, asked bluntly, "Sir, you teaching us?" It was by no means a simple question, as it was tinged with incredulity and non-acceptance. Nevertheless, within a few weeks, we had bonded as teacher and students. I enjoyed the classes and I could tell that they did too. It was clear that students appreciated teachers who cared and who took the time to help them.

The students in this class at Ellerslie were exceptional, and it was rewarding to see the positive results of our mutual efforts. Throughout my teaching career, I drew heavily from my experience in the Cadet Corps and employed the methods of instruction and people-management I had learnt as an instructor in the Barbados Cadet Corps. Cadet training served me well.

PO Edwin Millington

My love for the school and the students was such that in the early 1980s, I drove a team of senior cadets to Ellerslie every Tuesday afternoon to assist Sgt. Randolph Bourne and Sgt. Presteen Sobers after their unit was formed. PO Edwin Millington, who worked with me recently at Cadet Headquarters, was one of the cadets who benefitted from that gesture. He continues to speak about it, and remind me of the experience and what it meant to him.

Capt. Randolph Charles

Very often we do what is necessary at the time and then forget about it because we did not do it for recognition or praise. However, a reminder from someone who benefitted from our actions helps us to understand the impact we had on the lives of others and gives us the satisfaction of knowing that we made a difference. I am proud of the commitment of the Ellerslie School cadets, who went on to serve in the military, namely: PO Edwin Millington, Lt. (CG) John Walcott, Capt. Randolph Charles, Lt. (CG) Brian Roberts, Lt. Charles

Lt (CG) John Walcott

Bellamy, OCdt. Adrian Maloney and others who ensured that the fledgling Number 4 Cadet Company at Ellerslie did not fail.

I am even more pleased that at least three of these Ellerslie cadets: Lt (CG) John Walcott, Capt. Randolph Charles and PO Edwin Millington returned to serve in the Barbados Cadet Corps.

These Ellerslie Cadets knew that they were members of a Newer Secondary School entering an organization previously dominated by students from three Older Secondary Schools. They had to ensure that they set a high standard and that the experiment of including Ellerlie School as the fourth Cadet Company did not fail. This is exactly what they did. I was standing at the St. Lucy Depot that morning in July 1979 when they got off the bus to start their very first camp – Basic Training camp. When they fell in and marched onto the parade square, the precision of their drill and the pride, exhibited said to us that they were going to be a force to be reckoned with.

From 1975-1979, I got an opportunity to work alongside "the great triumvirate of the 1970's," Lt. Maynard, Capt. Ron Clarke (deceased) and Capt. Carroll Mapp (deceased). They were a powerful team of leaders. Although each man looked after the interests of his unit, they all contributed to the Corps as a whole.

Lt. Maynard excelled on the parade square and in executing training modules. Capt. Mapp was a good administrator and handled exams very efficiently, while Capt. Clarke was very keen on setting up ranges and organizing shoots and social activities. They loved the Cadet Corps. They worked in harmony and never showed differences of opinion openly. They were always present when their cadets were in camp, and would only leave to participate in exercises. This is why I referred to them as "the great Triumvirate of the 1970s."

Although I was studying for a degree in modern languages at the University of The West Indies, I was able to attend summer camps from 1976 – 1978. I was involved in the camp in St. Vincent (July 1975), St Lucia (August 1977) and at home at St Ann's Fort (August 1978).

In the camp at St. Ann's Fort, I witnessed the "Passing Out Parade" for the Ellerslie school cadets. This was the formal inauguration of that unit. I witnessed the pride of the students, the Principal, the teachers, the parents

Sgt. John Walcott of the Ellerslie Cadet Company

and, of course, the senior non-commissioned officers attached to the group. Sergeants Presteen Sobers and Randolph Bourne, both dedicated and passionate leaders, guided this new unit into becoming the first to be formed at a secondary school in seventy-four years. This brought the total number of cadet units to four. On that occasion, the cadets of the No.4 Company paraded in physical training gear - white shirt and blue trousers. Later they wore khaki shirts, long khaki trousers and blue and gold stable belts – a uniform which was similar to that worn only by the Band and Drums of No.3 Company. All other cadets wore short khaki pants at that stage.

With all of these experiences, I was being slowly initiated into a leadership role in the Corps, and there was much more orientation to come.

14

Initiation into Planning and Management of Overseas Camps

My friend Charles White relaxing aboard the Federal Maple.

Dominica Camp 1974

I was fortunate to be involved in three overseas camps in the Caribbean, both as a senior cadet and as an adult leader.

I have always thought that it took a strong and courageous leader to try what others do not dare to try. I cannot say exactly what motivated Lieutenant Maynard to plan an overseas camp in Dominica in 1974, but I can guess that it was for the sake of keeping the cadets motivated. After 1973, when the Canadian/Caribbean exchange ended abruptly, opportunities for travel in the Cadet Corps were non-existent, and numbers dwindled.

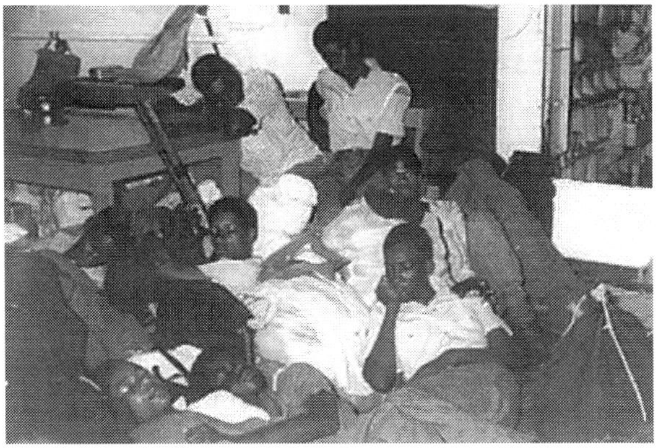

Seated (in white lanyard) among cadets sleeping on board the Federal Maple en route to St. Lucia and Dominica, 1974.

It was also the era of the afro hairstyle and, again, this was a challenge for an organization which demanded that hair be trimmed a quarter inch at the sides and back of the head. The promise of an overseas camp was the glue which kept the No 3. Company together.

I was intrigued with the level of planning involved in making the trip a reality. The key area was financing. Lt. Maynard needed to find an inexpensive means of transport. The plane from Barbados to Dominica could only carry half of the cadets, and we needed to find a mode of transportation to carry them all at once. Fortunately, there was the Federal Maple, one of two ships sailing through the Caribbean daily, and the necessary arrangements were made to transport the cadets by sea.

The day came when we boarded the Federal Maple with just over sixty cadets, including the lone female, Margot Greene. In those days, there were very few parents seeing us off - a total contrast to what happens today, where many parents are able to witness the departure of their children. Our parents knew that they would not see or hear from us until we returned home. Today, parents get instant feedback about the arrival of their children overseas. Sometimes it was necessary to control this activity. There were times when parents overreacted to information from their children about food and facilities. Naturally, circumstances will differ wherever you go, but travel teaches us how to adapt to varying cultures and ways of life. This learning experience can be spoiled when people expect conditions to be the same as they are in their own country.

The vessel left for Dominica via St. Lucia. When we disembarked, we walked through the streets of Castries, and all the buildings seemed to be moving like a see-saw. Clearly, we were still feeling the effects of the rocking boat. We spent an entire day in Castries before leaving for Dominica at nightfall.

We slept on an open deck, which allowed for laughter, jokes and a body-building competition, all of which would have been impossible had we travelled by plane.

1974:Cpl Charles White, Drum Major David Straughan and the author share a light-hearted moment with LCpl Lashley and Cpl Lascelles of the Barbados Regiment at Camp Londonderry.

On reaching Dominica, a police launch transported us to the jetty. Once assembled, we were taken to a nearby building for refreshments before heading to Camp Londonderry, which was some distance away from Roseau.

On the journey to Camp Londonderry, and throughout the Dominica experience, I noted how thoroughly Lt. Maynard had planned. Everything fitted into place. Everything worked like clockwork. I assumed that he had done a recce in advance of our visit. This was the type of approach I adopted later in my career.

Camp Londonderry was an excellent campsite. The Dominican cadets who joined us enhanced the experience. Major Johnson, who was the Commandant of the Dominica Cadet Corps, was particularly hospitable, and so too was Lieutenant Ackroyd Burmingham. In the group of cadets, were two people who would later become very dear friends of mine - Francis Richards, who later became Commandant, and Gabriel Christian, who is now a lawyer in Maryland, USA.

Combermere display team marching along the streets of Roseau towards Goodwill Pasture.

Some of the main attractions in Dominica were the rivers, grapefruit and banana plantations, the mountains and the vegetation, all of which combined to provide an excellent training environment.

Drum Major David Straughan leads Band and infantry through the streets of Roseau.

We did a precision drill display on Goodwill Pasture in Roseau for the Dominican public. I was the Parade Commander and the Parade Sergeant Major was Cpl. Harland Lascelles of the Barbados Regiment, who was given that appointment for camp. This display squad was excellent and created quite a stir among the on-lookers.

The combined band of Barbadian and Dominican cadets played some melodious tunes. Drum Major David Straughan, who had done a "crash course" in carrying the mace, gave a performance which I have hardly even seen equalled in all the years that I have been associated with the Barbados Cadet Corps.

Cpl. Lascelles was one of the most outstanding instructors to ever work with the Cadet Corps. He understood what unit commanders were trying to achieve and played his part, even if it meant allowing me, a school boy, to play the role of officer with him as Sergeant Major under my command. Such humility could have easily been overlooked, but I cannot forget his genuine desire to guide me.

When I became Officer Commanding No. 3 Company, I relied heavily on him in matters of drill and ceremony. He was a tower of strength to our organization. In Dominica in 1974, he created the buzz words "Work Hard." Everyone caught that vision and worked accordingly.

Lt. Maynard would have been conscious that one of his predecessors had also planned and executed a camp in Dominica. In 1939, Combermere cadets were taken to Dominica by Capt. Ralph Perkins, whom I later met as my second form English teacher. In 1960, it was Mr. Charlie Pilgrim's turn as Officer Commanding and he accompanied cadets to St. Lucia. This group included the now Colonel H.D. Maynard.

Barbados Cadet Corps Camps Overseas

The success of the 1974 trip by No. 3 Company to Dominica seemed to have galvanized Nos. 1 and 2 companies into action. As a result, in 1975 and 1977, the entire Barbados Cadet Corps held camps in St. Vincent and St. Lucia respectively.

Cadets on board the Seimstrand, 1975.

St Vincent Camp 1975

This St. Vincent trip was special. Instead of camping in Barbados, all resources were funneled into the effort to stage a camp in St. Vincent. Barbados Regiment personnel who accompanied the group included Sgt. Major Agard (Armourer), Cpls. Lascelles, Beckles, John Brathwaite, Hackett and a medic, Pte. Carrington.

It was also a trip in which females participated in larger numbers than they had in Dominica.

The campsite was at Prospect House, and personnel travelled by two separate vessels. A team, led by Captain Carroll Mapp comprising Barbados Regiment support staff, left Barbados two days in advance to prepare the campsite. Travelling aboard the Seimstrand, we arrived only a few hours after they did, as their vessel, I am told, had drifted off course.

As is customary for overseas camps of this nature, there was a ceremonial parade held in Kingstown. Many Vincentians came out to see their own cadets on parade, which was reviewed by the Premier, the Hon. Milton Cato.

The Combermere Cadet Band playing music for the parade in Kingstown, St. Vincent.

Prime Minister Hon. Milton Cato takes the salute.

The Author Commanding Combermere Detachment in St. Vincent.

Another memorable event was a church parade in nearby Calliaqua. The band and cadets from the three units set off at 6:30 a.m. on a march for church service, which was scheduled to start at 7:00 a.m.

The Commandant of the St. Vincent Cadet Corps and his officers were very supportive.

St. Lucia Camp 1977

Numbers in the unit began to swell with these overseas camps. The strategy was reaping dividends. Hence, a second overseas camp was planned for 1977. This time, the target country was St. Lucia and the campsite was on the Morne - a location which is now an educational complex. Cpl. Lascelles, Pte. Dennis Browne, as medic and Sgt. Major Agard, as Armourer, were the staff sent from the Barbados Regiment. We travelled by the Vengsoy.

One of the highlights of the St. Lucia camp was a mini display of "Trooping the Colours" held in Castries.

Another memorable activity was the "Exercise Pipeline," an expedition held on the penultimate day of the camp. By the time the cadets returned, they were so exhausted that the debriefing session had to be postponed.

These experiences were the stepping stones for my duty as Staff Officer Cadets and Cadet Executive Officer. My camping experiences in the Caribbean highlighted the goodwill of people in Guyana, Dominica, St. Vincent and St. Lucia, who displayed true neighbourly behavior.

I was determined to repay this debt of gratitude some time in the future, but first I had to complete my university degree, apply for a job at Combermere and, hopefully, be taken on staff.

Barbadian Cadets at the Morne campsite.

Trooping The Colour.

15

Twice a Teacher

Posing (Front row, left) with members of staff on a special day when teachers dressed as students

Returning from Trinidad in 1979, I was honoured and humbled to be asked to join the staff at Combermere to teach Spanish.

I was pleased that the Headmaster and other school authorities thought that I would be an asset to the school, as there were others who could have filled the post. I was thankful for the opportunity and determined to "give back" to my students what was given to me and, possibly, more abundantly!

I started teaching modern languages at Combermere in 1979 and thoroughly enjoyed the dual role of teacher and cadet officer. Teaching is a vocation. One has to like it to be successful. I wanted to be a teacher from since I was in the fourth form. I had observed the various styles of teachers and decided how I wanted to be as a teacher. I wanted to make an impact in the lives of my students, but some friends told me not to waste my ability by being a teacher. But I ignored them because there was something compelling me to teach.

I am glad that I followed my inclination. I have had the greatest satisfaction from teaching and then switching to the role of cadet officer after school. In every sense, I was twice a teacher; working in the classroom between 8:30 a.m. and 3:00 p.m. and then being involved with some aspect of cadet training in the afternoon. Recruit training took place on Tuesday afternoons, and meetings of NCOs could easily occur on Mondays or Wednesdays. The cadet band practiced on Wednesdays, followed by regular parade on Fridays and shooting practice at 6 o'clock the next morning. On Saturdays just after Shooting practice, Cadet Band practice was held. On Sundays, the band would, from time to time, perform at a church or at a social activity. Therefore, my leisure time outside of teaching was totally consumed by cadet corps activities.

Col. Maynard, Acting Chief of Staff with Commandant Lt. Col. Owen Springer and Parade Commander, Captain James Bradshaw with sword in hand.

It was not long before Lt. Maynard informed me that he intended to join the Regular Army. The BDF had just been established, and he wanted to contribute to its development. He was grooming me for leadership as Officer Commanding.

He explained to me that it was important to move on because a person becomes predictable over a period of time and, therefore, not as effective. That was difficult to understand in his case because he had always seemed so full of ideas. However, his departure was inevitable.

Lt. Maynard was soon promoted to the rank of Captain and eventually retired as Colonel and Chief of Staff of the BDF.

The prospect of taking over command was daunting, given that it was such a large company and that the predecessor appeared larger than life to us. I could have refused, but I chose to accept the position of Officer Commanding, albeit with a tinge of trepidation.

16

My First Command

Standing in front of Combermere School in Barbados Regiment uniform.

There are some people who, on taking up a position, try to change everything that was done before in order to stamp their own authority. However, I recognized that there were many things which worked well, and should be maintained. Nevertheless, we all have our own perspectives on life, and although we make changes as we see fit, we always have to be careful not to change too many things too quickly. Followers are often unable to cope with rapid and constant change.

I plunged right into the role of Officer Commanding No. 3 Company, Barbados Cadet Corps and tried to maintain the standards set. There were many exciting activities during that period. We continued the weekend hikes and bivouacking at locations around the island, including Congo Bay, River Bay, and Archer's Bay and the East Coast Road. These activities were successful. With the Principal's permission, cadets would leave at the end of school on Friday evenings and hike to an intermediary point. They would spend the night at that location and then move to the final destination. I would have selected grid reference locations on the coast line as final bivouac points and some intermediary points which they were required to reach on the first night.

Battle PT for advanced level cadets.

We always sought permission from the owners of the properties to be occupied by Cadets. Platoons would meet to decide on the best course to take and what stores and resources they would need. In those days, school units were relatively self-sufficient and the process worked very well.

Hike to Gun Hill.

I used to make arrangements for the Barbados Regiment to send two open-back trucks to collect the cadets on the Sunday afternoon. The cadets were given the coordinates for the pickup points and the four platoons were expected to rendezvous at two points, with two platoons meeting at each point.

There were times during the year when we conducted shorter hikes, like the one done to Gun Hill. Cadets left Combermere early in the morning, hiked to Gun Hill and took part in practical map reading activities before returning to school that same afternoon.

There were also annual ceremonial parades, especially for Speech Day and at Independence time. Each year, the senior cadets wanted to perform more challenging parade maneuvers. As a result, in 1981, we did a semi Trooping the Colours as part of the Independence celebrations. It was considered one of the more complicated routines, and we received very good reviews.

A big hit with the school and the cadets was the inter-platoon drill competition held mainly in the second term, when other activities were overshadowed by athletics. I needed a solution to maintain interest in "cadetting," and the drill competition, together with an inter-platoon cross-country run, seemed the perfect answer.

1981: No. 3 Company Trooping the Colour

The drill competition was held during an entire week, with three platoons and the band drawing, lottery-style, for which days they would be "on stage." The competition was held in the car park/parade square half an hour before school started.

Inspection of Drill Team.

Students responded very well to the spectacle, aligning themselves with their favourite platoons and cheering for them from the sidelines. Judged by BDF personnel, the competition lasted for the first four days and the winning platoon was announced on the Friday.

Corporals and Lance Corporals having lunch.

There were also daily luncheons held during Cadet Week, in which different ranks within the company were treated to lunch, paid for by the cadets. The groups comprised officers, senior non-commissioned officers, corporals, lance corporals and cadets. When it was the cadets' turn to be treated, they were served by the officers and SNCOs. Naturally, the luncheons were much appreciated by the cadets.

I was ably assisted in these ventures by Officer Cadet Vernon Leacock. He was a math teacher at the school, who had been a cadet in the Harrison College's No. 1 Company. He was very thorough in accounting for equipment and stores and provided good support as a second-in-command. His understanding of the need for good safety practices among cadets was important to me.

CUO Derek Haynes preparing a shooting team at the start of range practice, 1981.

One of the most significant achievements of No. 3 Company during my tenure as Officer Commanding was winning the Martinez Shooting Trophy in its final year (1981). The team of dedicated cadets practiced long hours to regain the trophy, which Combermere had not won since 1968.

On Saturday mornings, as early as 6:30, we gathered for practice at the shooting range at Combermere. The group included Marlon Best, who went on to shoot competitively for Barbados; Ricardo Vickers, who is now a senior BDF officer; Kurtley Archer, who has retired from the BDF; Derek Haynes; Festus Etienne; David Batson; and Ian Arthur.

Those were the days when there were rifles in the armoury at Combermere and the officer commanding had full control of shooting arrangements. Drill purpose weapons were on loan for an entire school term, and the three older secondary schools had purchased their own .22 caliber rifles. Therefore, I could organize shooting practices because the rifles were in the armoury. Over time, security considerations changed this arrangement. Moreover, the Martinez Competition was also discontinued.

As Officer Commanding No. 3 Company, I knew I also had a responsibility to help other units. I was taught by my parents to share and I saw this assistance as sharing resources. I have already mentioned the help given to Ellerslie Secondary where I took a Cadet Under Officer, a Sergeant Major and two other instructors from Combermere to Ellerslie in my personal vehicle every Tuesday evening to assist with training, in support of the efforts of Sgt. Randolph Bourne and Sgt. Presteen Sobers. I also assisted the Louis Lynch Cadet Company when the then Capt. Clyde Parris was in charge of that unit, by allowing them to join No. 3 Company for training on evenings for a period of time.

Eartha and author on our wedding day with Best Man, L.t Col. Jeffrey Bostic at left and dad Reuben St. Cyr at right.

In my book "The Combermere Cadet," I wrote about a number of Combermerians who served in the military. Since then, a significant number of cadets who were under my command rose to high ranks within the Barbados Defence Force. Current officers include Commander Ricardo Shurland, Major Ricardo Vickers and Major Glyne Grannum. Lt. Col. Jeffrey Bostic, who was Best Man at my wedding in 2003, when I married the former Eartha St. Cyr, is currently the Parliamentary Representative for the City of Bridgetown, and Lt. Col. Clyde Parris, works for the United Nation in Papua New Guinea. Whenever he returns to Barbados, he always comes to visit me.

Author congratulating CUO Derek Haynes for his team's performance in winning the Martinez Trophy

When the BDF was established in 1979, the Combermere Cadet Company was thriving under the leadership of the then Lieutenant Maynard. When he left Combermere and joined the BDF Regular Force, I continued the process of building No. 3 Company. It was not surprising then that many of the senior cadets, seeing a future in gaining full-time employment, joined the BDF. Thirty-three years later, some of them still hold those positions of authority.

The unconditional friendships which I share with all those officers started from those early days at Combermere when I was Officer Commanding that unit.

SLt Derek Haynes in the BDF Officers' Mess

Many of the cadets also assumed responsibilities in civilian organizations, including Derek Haynes, a faithful ex-Combermerian, who often returns to Barbados for the annual school reunion in October. I did not have enough details about him at the time of writing my first book and, hence, I am very glad to be able to share his story with the public now.

2nd Lt Haynes in his flying suit at 3CFFTS.

While at Combermere, he reached the rank of Sergeant Major - a signature and defining rank in the cadets/military. He finished his career as a Cadet Under Officer of No. 3 Company, which is also a prestigious rank within the Barbados Cadet Corps.

In addition, he played the clarinet and the saxophone in the Combermere Cadet Band.

He joined the Barbados Defence Force and was attached to the Barbados Coast Guard, where he achieved the rank of Sub-Lieutenant, while completing his pilot's training. Derek attended flight school in Canada, and was particularly proud that he was one of only three BDF officers to have done a military pilot's training course.

Derek at LIAT

Senior First Officer Derek Haynes, who is now a pilot with Virgin Atlantic Airways on the Airbus A340-600, had this to say in an email to me: "I know that many people contribute to where you find yourself, but had you not convinced me to interview/join the BDF, I probably wouldn't be flying today. Thank you, Sir."

Senior First Officer Derek Haynes in the cockpit of the Airbus A340-600

Derek is expecting to fly the Boeing 787 Dreamliner when Virgin Atlantic takes delivery of them in October 2014

This note from Derek is, for me, the special reward which a teacher or Cadet Corps Officer enjoys receiving. We are proud of the successes of our students. It is even more special when they pause to recognize the effort which we have put in. Teaching is not an easy job. Also, compensation does not match effort. But our students keep us motivated, especially when we know that our work is not in vain and our advice is well taken. I actively chose to teach and I was fortunate to meet some fine young men and women as students and they have, in many ways, enriched my own life.

When we were training our cadets, we did not know what their status in life would be. We just wanted to produce young men and women with the qualities that would benefit them and their country, regardless of their chosen profession. We wanted to provide them with the skills to fit into society and to make a difference in the lives of those around them. By extension, we were enhancing the social fabric of our country and preparing our students to reach out to the world in confidence. This was our legacy in the Cadet Corps.

Major Deighton Maynard with outstanding senior Cadets from Combermere School. (Left to right) CSM Ricardo Shurland, 2Lt Jeffrey Bostic, 2Lt Kurtley Archer, Major Deighton Maynard, CUO Randolph Sandiford, CUO Kirk Taitt, and CUO Gay Griffith

17

Part of a Proud Tradition

I am always conscious that I am part of a long and proud line of educators who felt that sacrificing their leisure time to be leaders in the Cadet Corps, was an important "hobby." Some people choose hobbies which provide relaxation and distraction from their work. The reverse is true with this particular hobby, where the "fun" comes from spending long hours grappling with the problems of our youth. Quite often, relaxation was out of the question. What a strange hobby.

I have always admired the first Commandant of the Barbados Cadet Corps, Captain Radcliffe Hall, who was a teacher at The Lodge School, and an officer in the Barbados Volunteer Force. People like him, saw the Cadet Corps as an important addition to the schools' curriculum, providing leadership for young school boys.

We have come a long way since the Corps comprised only boys. It now includes girls and is accessible to students from every secondary school in Barbados. But the founding principles guided me.

I sought throughout the years to emphasize that the Cadet Corps was simply an extra-curricular activity meant to develop strength of character in children.

My response was always, "We provide training for students to be the most disciplined doctors, janitors, artisans or whichever profession they choose. However, if they want a career in the army or police force, they would have already developed the basic military skills on which to build that career." My counterparts in the Caribbean, United Kingdom and Canada, with whom I interacted, expressed the same view – even those from the British Army Cadet Force, with its strong ties to the army. My point is that the training done is simply a vehicle for developing self-control and qualities of good citizenship.

Capt. Radcliffe Hall, the founder of the Cadet Corps at The Lodge School wrote in the Lodge School Record (vol. V11, 1913), pp. 16 – 22):

The Lodge School Cadets 1907

> Twenty years ago, Englishmen arriving in Barbados and coming into more or less contact with the Public School boys of little England were struck with the close similarity in the matter of school work and scholarship between the boys of this and the Mother Country, and equally forcibly with the lamentable lack of a proper school discipline......
>
> It was late in 1903 that Mr. Emtage, Headmaster of The Lodge School considered that the psychological moment had arrived and approached the Science master, who was also an Officer of the Barbados Volunteer Force, with the suggestion that the time had come to try to develop, if not a regular cadet company, at any rate a Drill squad. After discussion as to ways and means and as to what system would be most advantageous in all respects, a start was made, Mr. R. Hall only too ready and willing to start.

From as early as 1899, boys were being drilled at Combermere School twice a week by a drill instructor from the Barbados Volunteer Force, but Combermere did not establish a Cadet Unit until 1904. The Headmaster of that era, Mr. George Burton would, no doubt, have played his part in seeing the company become a reality in 1904.

When I became a cadet in 1971, extra-curricular activities were highly regarded. "Cadetting," scouts and sports were actual subjects on the timetable. The last two periods on Fridays were dedicated to these

Combermere School Shooting Team. Headmaster, Mr. Burton seated proudly among his cadets, 1912.

1983. Author speaking to Mr. Charlie Pilgrim, Principal (extreme right) as OC No.3 Company (Extreme Left): Mr. Keith Roach, Deputy Principal and Guide leader Mrs. Marva Lahai.

"subjects." This was before other subjects began to take precedence and these activities were removed from the formal curriculum and relegated to after school hours.

Cadet training was intended to use military discipline in the development of character. Punctuality, respect for authority, physical and mental endurance, teamwork and pride and industry were some of the attributes which were stressed. These were considered vital elements of good citizenship, which surpassed the boundary of military service. These were values which were not easily taught in the formal classroom setting. This was why the Barbados Cadet Corps had been the ideal training ground for generations of Barbadian youths and their counterparts from other countries.

The key factor which has led to the success of the Barbados Cadet Corps is the unwavering support of Principals of schools. One Principal was actually Officer Commanding No. 3 Company before he became Principal. That was Mr. Charlie Pilgrim. Successive Headmasters understood the value of the Cadet Corps in a school and this is the essential reason why the Corps thrived at Combermere School and at the other two units.

1960 Headmaster, Major Cecil Noott watches on as Lt. Charlie Pilgrim (OC No. 3 Company) accompanies the Inspecting Officer.

I believe that we must continually emphasize the underlying reasons behind what is done in the Cadet Corps. The onlooker sees only marching, cadets shouting orders, crawling on the ground, swimming, or engaging in a range of activities associated with the various branches of the Barbados Cadet Corps. Those people, who were around in 1981, would know the popular calypso "Boots" by The Mighty Gabby. It spoke of "Boots, boots boots and more boots marching..." I have always stressed that cadet training involves more than just boots and marching.

There are so many attributes acquired from "cadetting" – respect for authority, self-reliance, and physical and mental endurance, to name a few.

Cadets are taught to aim for excellence and to take pride in whatever they do. Excellence is about doing something at the best possible level of efficiency. In the Cadet Corps, cadets practice drill movements and other skills repeatedly. When they think they have done it well enough, they are usually told, "Let's rehearse again." They are taught to not accept mediocre performances, knowing that these lessons would help them develop a sense of diligence and commitment to whatever task they are assigned.

There is always a need for someone who is a standard setter in our society. Cadet training is designed to teach the cadets that each of them could, in their own way, be standard setters, displaying correct behavior. They are taught that a good reputation matters, and that apart from qualifications, prospective employers want to know something about their character. The former Commandant of Dominica Cadet Corps, Major Francis Richards, explained it this way, "Two students come to you for a job. One has academics or vocational qualifications only in one pocket. The cadet turns up with a set of qualifications in both pockets. He has academic or vocational qualifications in the left pocket and he has all the skills learnt from cadet training in the right pocket or vice versa. What are these skills? They are punctuality, respect for authority, physical and mental endurance and good manners."

Those are best summed up in an acronym introduced by the Right Reverend Sir Wilfred Wood, a former Combermere cadet. Sir Wilfred was addressing the Combermere church service to mark the centenary of the unit in 2004. He used the concept of a DART with its sharp point aimed carefully at a target. I wish to share a few thoughts using this acronym.

The essential ingredients for excellence start with the letter D.

***D* is for Discipline.** In the Cadet Corps, discipline is intended to lead to self-control. On the Independence Day Parade, when I was a cadet, I remember that the rain fell on a number of occasions, and at least three times our uniforms dried on parade. No one flinched. That discipline taught us to cope with tough circumstances in life.

Nevertheless, I am ambivalent towards the whole question of discipline. I know the difference between discipline, which is intended for a positive outcome and that which amounts to an abuse of authority.

On the morning of the Independence Day Parade in 1972, as young cadets we witnessed a classic example of abuse of authority, which might be mistaken for discipline by the person who committed the act. The parade was being held at the National Stadium for the first time and we stood rigidly in the ranks and executed our drill with pride, trying very hard not to "fall out," despite not having had any breakfast.

In those days, we slept in the barracks at St. Ann's Fort the night before important national parades. On this occasion, there was only a small full-time staff in the Barbados Regiment and therefore, there was adequate accommodation for cadets from the three companies.

In the morning, just before the parade, we would go to the mess kitchen located outside the Officers' Mess to have coffee. On the morning in question, the line was long and cadets were chatting, while inching forward. Suddenly, and to everyone's surprise, a Warrant Officer who was supervising this activity, became angry, took up the percolator and emptied the coffee onto the floor. Our hearts sank. We would not have had anything to eat or drink since the night before when we had supper.

Then we were told to "fall in" to be transported by bus to the stadium. We were determined not to faint although our stomachs were empty. I never understood the outburst, and I have seen other senseless deeds by others, which have prompted me to ask, "Who will guard the guards?" I remembered my first lecture on leadership which stressed that we ought to be firm, fair and, yet, friendly. I thought, with some amusement, that perhaps some leaders missed that class. I realized then, at that tender age, that accountability only works if people in senior positions are truly held to account.

A is for Accountability. Everyone is accountable for his or her actions. For some people, accountability means saying "yes" to those ranked above them in the chain of command, and "no" to those ranked below. Some people work very hard or pretend to work very hard when superiors are around, but do little or no work when no one in authority is present. Cadet training teaches cadets that they are accountable. The Orders Process, where cadets are brought before a senior officer in a very formal setting to be interviewed for outstanding efforts or to hear accusations against them, provides a clear understanding that there are both rewards and punishments. Typically, punishment would be meted out for failure to perform a duty, absence without excuse or conduct unbecoming of a cadet.

R is for Respect. The cadet is taught that the uniform of any great organization commands respect. The Cadet Corps in Barbados is now 108 years old. One of our governors-general, several ministers of-government, leaders in businesses and many prominent individuals in our society have served as cadets. Uniforms encourage cadets to live up to high expectations. This starts with cleaning and preparation. For example, cadets spend long hours "water shining" the tips of their boots. The neater the cadet is dressed, the greater the image of the Barbados Cadet Corps is enhanced.

Cadets are often held to a higher standard of behavior, and that is as it should be. The training cadets receive should make them develop greater respect for authority and for other people around them. Lack of respect can ruin a society.

T is for Teamwork. Cadets learn that in any military or civilian organization, there are a number of different, but complimentary roles. We emphasize that "Corps" is a French word for "body," and remind them that if any member of the body is not functioning, then the entire body will not work well. The French phrase "esprit de corps," speaks to this concept. Translated, it means literally "spirit of body," but is another way of saying "team spirit." Cadets learn that everyone is important in the chain of command. They learn that there can be only one commanding officer; one prime minister; or one captain of a football team. But they all have to work together to be successful.

The Cadet Corps continues to place great emphasis on encouraging young people to function as teams rather than as selfish individuals. The Corps helps them to understand that regardless of their job, they are part of the corps of society. There is no "I" in the word TEAM, which could be an acronym for **T**-Together; **E**-Everyone; **A**-Achieves; **M**-More.

As trainers and leaders of young people and the entire society, we must ask ourselves what type of Barbados do we want to live in; what do we want to leave for our children and grandchildren? Then we must make every effort to train them. We cannot get away from the biblical scripture, "Train up the children in the way they should go." We must teach them to aim for excellence in school work just as we aim a dart at a target, hoping that it hits the centre and scores the most points. We must not allow their behavior to lapse or leave their progress to chance.

These reflections reminded me of the true purpose of my commitment. Successive Cadet Corps leaders have had to help authorities understand that the Cadet Corps was not a nursery for the military, but an important aspect of the school's programme for character-building. I crusaded for that level of acceptance and never waivered.

PART 2

18

A Renewed Call to Service

My father died on 18th August 1993. Not having fully recovered from this sharp blow, I also suffered another whiplash with the passing of my mother in quick succession. Within four weeks, I had lost both parents. On the day my mother passed away, I received a visit from the then Lt. Col Maynard, Deputy Chief of Staff of the Barbados Defence Force. It was his official responsibility to console me. I found solace in spending that entire period talking about the Cadet Corps. He indicated that the BDF was setting up a new headquarters and that he thought I could contribute. I expressed interest noting, however, that I would need to spend the school term from September to December with my sixth and fifth form students.

A few days after my mother died, students from the fifth form called to invite me to a restaurant to spend time with them. When I arrived, there were about twenty students waiting for me, and I was overwhelmed by their show of support. They just sat with me and helped me to bear my sorrow, especially after having lost both my father and mother in the space of four weeks. Given this rapport with my students, I felt it necessary to request a delay in accepting the post at the new Cadet Headquarters. My students were always special to me and I thought that I needed to prepare them as much as possible for their exams.

Thankfully, the request was accepted by the then Chief of Staff, Brigadier Rudyard Lewis and, by January 1994, I was installed as Staff Officer Cadets. This was the first time that a teacher / cadet officer had been given such an opportunity. I may have been the natural choice, as there was only Capt. Ron Clarke who remained from among the original officers of the 1970s and he was serving as Deputy Headmaster of Harrison College. Both Lt. Maynard and Capt. Mapp had taken up appointments in the Barbados Defence Force, and the remaining officers were quite junior.

Once again, my former teacher and Officer Commanding, who had always influenced the course of my life, was encouraging me along a path of service. I knew it was going to be a very important stage of my life,

Seven years before I was posted to the new Cadet Headquarters, the Barbados Defence Force reintroduced the system from 1904. This system put school teachers in charge of cadet units after receiving the necessary training in the Potential Officers' Course.

This followed an attempt to have BDF officers provide leadership for the Corps, but its rapid expansion between 1981 and 1982 resulted in a shortage of qualified adult personnel. The Defence Force initially sought to alleviate this problem by posting its regular officers to the various newly formed companies. By 1984, it was clear that this system was inadequate. The qualifying course for potential officers from Barbados, St. Lucia and St. Vincent was conducted by officers and non-commissioned officers from the Barbados Defence Force.

1984: Potential Cadet Officer Course students march past on the Closing Parade. Parade Commander is Second Lieutenant P Skeete.

The first Potential Officers were trained in 1984. This course was run by a BDF officer, Major Charles Brathwaite. I had the pleasure of being Parade Commander at their Passing Out Parade. This group included Major James Bradshaw, Major Irvin Boyce, Lt. Cdr. Carl Farley, the late Major Rawlston Nichols and the late Capt. Victor Etienne.

I resigned from the Barbados Defence Force that same year and spent the next seven years with my family, having been married in 1982 to the former Beverley Roberts. This was my first marriage. I resigned my commission in the BDF about two weeks after the birth of my first daughter, Gemma. Two other daughters, Alicia and Janelle came in quick succession. My responsibility as a father was, for me, of paramount importance.

Gemma, Janelle and Alicia with Principal, Ms. Marcia Watson, at Eden Lodge Nursery School.

Shortly after Gemma was born, Mr. Carl Wade, my former English teacher, pulled me aside one afternoon in the staff room and asked, "How old is your daughter?" I said, "Three months old." He advised me to start reading to her every night and, eventually, she would develop a love for reading. It seemed like obvious advice, but sometimes what is obvious is not always done. I trusted his judgment and started the process.

I read to her and my other two daughters every night, from their infancy until they developed a love for reading on their own. They would eventually read before going to bed. They would each borrow three books from the Public Library and would rotate them. Therefore they all read nine books each time. I also took them to nursery school, Eden Lodge Nursery School, and later to primary

My children playing in the garden with their cousins.

school. Eden Lodge Nursery gave all three of them an excellent start in their education, and we built a good rapport with the Principal, Ms. Marcia Watson and the staff. Gemma attended West Terrace Primary and later St. Stephen's Primary, while her sisters attended St. Stephen's Primary. They had excellent tuition at these institutions.

I served as treasurer and floor member on the parent teacher associations at the various schools my children attended over the years. My job as a teacher allowed me the opportunity to take them to school and collect them at the end of the day. The vacation periods gave me time to take them to the beach or play park, or sit on the lawn and watch them play with their cousins, Kay, Kevin and Kris (my sister Patricia's children) who lived next door and Gregory and Jeniece, my brother Steve's children.

A photo taken with my daughters around 2007.

I am glad now that I took the opportunity to spend time with them. They grew up so quickly and achieved some measure of success in their academic lives. Gemma is pursuing a career in the international business industry and Alicia is a certified accountant. Janelle is studying for a law degree.

Every seemingly adverse situation in life has a purpose. The conflicting requirements of an officer in the Barbados Defence Force and Officer Commanding of a large company constituted my initial reason for resigning. The requirements of the newly established BDF were different to those of the former Barbados Regiment. My service in the Cadet Corps, which involved activities almost every day of the week, was still seen as secondary to my responsibility as a BDF officer. I had to resign because I simply could not take on both responsibilities. However, it turned out to be a blessing, as I was able to spend long hours with my own children, at a critical stage in their lives.

Author standing in civilian clothing (extreme right) with the band.

Meanwhile, I continued to supervise the cadet band in the absence of a resident Officer Commanding at Combermere and provided guidance for ceremonies at the school.

It was difficult to be in the staff room at Combermere and to be on the outside of the Cadet Corps, but for those 7 years, I was still able to contribute by managing the cadet band, albeit in a civilian role. It was important to Combermere School and to the cadets that the band remained stable and functional.

Every Independence Day, I accompanied the band, in civilian clothing, to St. Ann's Fort, in the capacity of administrator.

It was against this backdrop that my appointment as Staff Officer Cadets was set. My appointment underscored the importance of having someone in the position who understood the school setting and had a military background. This was an unprecedented occurrence in the military in Barbados.

From my initial commitment to "giving back" to Combermere, my focus had broadened with this renewed call to service.

19

From Staff Officer Cadets to Cadet Executive Officer

When I undertook the position of Staff Officer Cadets, it was a distinct career change, but since it involved children and "cadetting," it seemed more of a hobby for me as previously mentioned.

I was initially taken on secondment for 2 years. Although the secondment meant that my job would still be waiting for me at Combermere, if I wanted to return, I endeavoured to do my best during that time. A line in my school song echoed in my mind "Truest highest fame lies in high endeavor." My Headmaster, Mr. C. Devere Moore, had written that sentence on my academic report every term for many years, as a source of inspiration and encouragement.

Being isolated in a room; answering the phone; attending meetings; planning and executing parades, luncheons and other Corps activities; were things I had to get used to. For years I had been standing in front of students, teaching Spanish, and my main resources were a blackboard, chalk and teaching materials.

My work assignment began on January 1, 1994 and was due to end in December 1996. I must have made a difference in my first two years, because, at the end of the secondment period, Brigadier Lewis requested that I remain for another year. He made similar requests for the next two years. Normally, people would go on secondment for two years and then return to their substantive posts. Sometimes they would spend three years. In my case, I was fortunate to have been granted five years of secondment.

In 1998, when Combermere's Board of Management advised that I could no longer be released for secondment, the BDF Headquarters recommended that I be appointed to the full-time post of Cadet Executive Officer. In January 1999, the appointment was confirmed. Although I was appointed by the Board and worked in the Cadet Corps, I held my appointment as a civilian.

To do my work effectively, I needed training and, luckily, was recommended for command and staff duties training. This course, held at the Paragon base of the Barbados Defence Force, was facilitated by the Regional Security System, of which Brigadier Lewis was the Regional Coordinator. The course lasted for six weeks and was an excellent introduction to command and staff duties. I benefitted immensely, and was particularly happy to be adjudged "Top Student".

As Cadet Executive Officer, I reported to the Cadet Commandant and was responsible for managing the daily activities. From time to time, there would be a meeting with the Chief of Staff and I accompanied him to those meetings.

In the early stages, life in Cadet Headquarters involved following a plan of scheduled events. However, as I became more settled, I recognized that there were a few areas which needed immediate attention. These included publicity; recruitment of adult leaders; establishment of units at the few remaining secondary schools; and the further development of the national band and sea cadet programmes. Sensitizing the principals, parents and guardians about the value of cadet training, and making the programme more interesting were on-going activities.

20

Development of Units

When I assumed the post of Staff Officer Cadets in 1994, there were eighteen cadet companies on record. It was clear that the Deighton Griffith, Alexandra and Alma Parris schools also needed units. Grantley Adams had had a unit, but it was dormant, as officers had transferred to other schools. At St. Lucy Secondary, there was a need for teachers to assist Capt. James Bradshaw.

The establishment of units was linked to recruitment of adult leaders, and to achieve this objective, I visited schools and consulted with the principals. I asked them if there were any young teachers, who would consider a career in the Cadet Corps. I asked permission to meet with them and do a presentation on the Cadet Corps. As a result of these visits, teachers from Alexandra (Captain Michael Boyce) and Alma Parris (Captain Naomi Williams) were identified. They remain officers in the Cadet Corps to this day.

In the case of the Deighton Griffith School, they had already met the requirements for the establishment of a unit and all that was needed was the administrative work. There were four adult leaders: Lieutenants Powlett and Walcott, 2Lt Amarel Collymore and 2Lt Andrew Skeete. There were also adequate numbers of boys and girls to commence training, and the school had made a secure office available to the unit. The Deighton Griffith School Unit was established in 1995, just one year after I became Staff Officer Cadets.

My attention was also focused on the cadet band. I had noticed that on Saturdays, an instructor, Mr. Simmons, a former member of the Barbados Regiment, came to Cadet Headquarters and was training about five cadets on the fife. Mr. Simmons was very dedicated and his efforts were appreciated. However, I had been told that the Cadet Corps had purchased a set of drums. Combermere's band was still active and The Lodge School and a few schools like Harrison College had excellent drum corps. It was evident that a fusion of these groups could be of great benefit to the Cadet Corps. Cadets could join what would be the national band, but still be available to their units for ceremonial parades.

The process of negotiating this arrangement started and, by November 1995 at Independence time, the National Cadet Band was formed. They were allowed to march unto the parade ground on Independence Day fifteen minutes before the start of the parade to play an interlude of music.

Independence Day 1995, the new National Cadet Band in their "Toy Soldier" uniforms.

The Cadet Band performing on the grounds of the Three W's Oval at the Cave Hill Campus, University of the West Indies.

The next step in the process was to find a leader for the band. The late Capt. Crofton Corbin had been designated Director of the Cadet Band, but he was also Director of the BDF band, which was very active at the time. I felt that, as usual, an officer/ teacher would be the ideal person.

My search took me to St. Leonard's Boys' School where a young man, Mr. Len Cummins, who had been a cadet at Combermere and a member of the band, was now a music teacher. After chatting with him briefly at the school, he agreed to sign up for recruitment as an officer and he completed the Potential Officers' Course in 1996. This decision was the start of many fruitful years for the Cadet Band under his baton. By the early 2000s, the band had competed in National Independence Festival of Creative Arts (NIFCA) and had won a Silver Award. This led to an invitation to give a special performance at the NIFCA Gala, where they slow-marched through the Garfield Sobers Gymnasium and onto the stage from both sides of the room to thunderous applause.

A few years before that performance, the band was featured at an Independence Day Parade. They played "Climb Every Mountain" from the "Sound Of Music," and went into a display of drums and sticks, perfected by drummers from The Lodge School, who were part of the National Band. The display thrilled everyone. I sat on the parade ground at the Garrison Savannah and savoured the routine, after which, Brigadier Lewis thanked them for their performance. He would no doubt have been very proud of them.

Sea cadet vessel.

Sea cadets testing their new boat.

A chance meeting with Mrs. Carolyn Troulan, a member of the British Women's Club at a party held by a friend, allowed me to discuss the Cadet Corps programme with her and her husband Jeremy. When they mentioned that they had sailed to Barbados some years ago, I suggested that they talk to our sea cadets about their experience. She thought the British Women's Club might be interested in our work with the cadets, and asked me to prepare a presentation on the Corps, to be delivered at their upcoming monthly meeting.

The members of the club were fascinated with the promotional video and PowerPoint presentation. They agreed to seek support through the Multinational Women's Forum for the cadet programme and were successful in gaining financial support for the band.

This new partnership allowed the band to receive much needed funds to purchase instruments from the now defunct Multinational Women's Forum. This was followed by another donation of funds from the Multinational Women's' Forum, to purchase a vessel for the sea cadets. Again, this was initiated by the British Women's Club, and we were extremely grateful for their generosity.

Cadet Band at BWU May Day march.

We also formed strong alliances with the Barbados Workers' Union (BWU). The BWU allowed us to use the training facilities at their Labour College at Mangrove, St. Philip.

In return, the Cadet Corps supported the union's May Day celebrations by sending the Cadet Band to head the

Members of the BWU and Social Partnership march behind the Cadet Band.

parade, which would usually start at the Garrison Savannah and end at Browne's Beach, via Culloden Road and Tweedside Road.

Annually, in January, cadets from the South Zone also took part in the Errol Barrow Day celebrations at the Barbados Workers' Union Labour College by providing a Guard of Honour.

The quest to establish partnerships to benefit the Corps was not written into any terms of reference, but seemed to me the best method of adding to limited resources.

21

Basic Officer Training

In order to maintain units, we had to recruit officers and train them. This was a relentless process.

Closing ceremony for Potential Officers' Course 2008.

From 1994 to 2000, I was fortunate to have the late Capt. Victor Etienne assisting me. He was a tremendous source of inspiration, and had previously served in the Barbados Defence Force Regular Army. He was one of my cadets at Combermere.

Victor was mentally sharp and understood the training requirements very well.

We shared the same barrack room during many of the Potential Officers' courses and spent hours at night discussing various aspects of training. Our philosophies on training coincided and many times he would write down a number of points which emerged from our conversations that he wanted to share with the other officers. These points eventually developed into a book.

One day, shortly before his death, he came to Cadet Headquarters and presented the manuscript to me. I thought that I owed it to him to have his work published, and after adding a number of chapters to the original document, I was able to have it published, with the support of the Government Printery. The book has since been used as a training resource for Potential officers.

We knew that we were not training our cadets to be soldiers. We felt that training adult leaders would provide them with military skills which were vital for working in a Cadet Corps environment and for conducting challenging and interesting activities for their cadets. However, we felt that the adults needed to understand why this training was necessary.

Following Victor's death, Capt. Dennis Browne assumed responsibility for the Potential Officers' Course, taking it to another level. His methodical approach was very impressive and students benefitted immensely from his vast experience.

Potential Officers' Course 1996

The Potential Officers' Course was an important part of training for Cadet Units of the Caribbean. Over the years, we had participation from Antigua, Dominica, St. Lucia, St. Vincent and the Grenadines, the Cayman Islands, Tortola, Grenada and Trinidad and Tobago.

One officer from Trinidad once told us that he considered the Barbados Cadet Corps to be the "Sandhurst of 'cadetting' in the Caribbean." Sandhurst is a prestigious military college in the United Kingdom and to have the comparison levelled at us was an accolade of the highest order.

Such was the impact of the course on students.

Potential Officers' Course (1998) was an important part of training for Cadet Units of the Caribbean.

22

Publicity

While we were dealing with the development of units and officers' training, we realized that underlying everything we sought to achieve was the dire need for publicity. The Cadet Corps was not as well-known as it ought to be, although it had been in existence in Barbados for more than nine decades.

One day I was in a bank and, as I filled out a form, the teller asked, "What is the Cadet Corps?" That question had been posed to me quite often, but this time it made me realize that we needed to address the matter of our visibility in the public arena.

It was felt that this could only be achieved through an aggressive publicity campaign. If the Corps was going to make an impact on local society, then it would be important for parents, guardians, schools and support organizations to understand what we were trying to achieve.

This is where the publicity campaign got its impetus. I often called the media to cover our activities, and CBC would usually carry the story on television. Among other activities, the public saw cadets marching, hiking and setting up bivouacs (small shelters in the field).

We also made good use of the Annual Principals' Conference, where I would capture various units' activities on video in five-minute clips to

Mr. Carl Padmore

Capt. Errol Brathwaite "The Chief"

demonstrate the progress we were making.

The most far reaching and exciting of the videos produced by the Corps was "Cadet Boot Camp," which was run at prime time as a twelve-week series on CBC television.

The series was the brainchild of Mrs. Suzanne Prescod of Saffire Productions – a former student of mine at Combermere School. It was a reality show – a competition in which the participants engaged in training activities done by the sea cadets, the infantry and the band. Each week, some of the participants who failed to complete tasks effectively were brought before "The Chief," a role played by our own Captain Errol Brathwaite. The sergeant in charge of training was Mr. "Alf" Padmore, a former cadet who is a well-known local comedian. His involvement was guaranteed to create interest.

The show started with ten participants, and each week, one of them was "booted off" the programme, hence the title: "Cadet Boot Camp."

Each programme featured both cadet activities and "Fact Files," which explained various aspects of the Corps. There were also occasions when the Commandant, Lt. Col. Trevor Browne, clarified some facet of the training. The overall prize for the winner was valued at BD$6,000. The series was also shown throughout the Caribbean on "Caribvision," and on subsequent visits to St. Lucia and St. Vincent, people on the streets who saw our uniform would shout out, "Cadet Boot Camp!"

We also took a film team to St. Vincent and St. Lucia in 2005 to capture our overseas camps. These trips resulted in a half-hour video production titled, "Connecting with our Caribbean Neighbours." Once again, it was shown in prime time on CBC.

Star 2 and 3 Cadets engaged in "exercise Back on Track" at Farley Hill, getting ready for their work in Disaster-preparedness

The following year 2006 on Independence Day, we again featured the Barbados Cadet Corps on CBC television. This time the focus was on Disaster-Preparedness and Saffire Productions were once again responsible for producing this show for television. This filming was done in Farley Hill and in Diamond Corner, St. Peter. The exercise, which was code-named "Exercise: Back on Track" involved Star 2 and 3 cadets.

At Independence time in 2007, CBC viewers were treated to a special half-hour programme featuring our inaugural International Cadet Challenge Camp (ICCC).

Competitors in the International Challenge Camp, 2007.

It was produced by Merville Lynch Productions with sponsorship from local companies, including The Barbados Light and Power Company Limited, Simpson Motors, United Insurance, Williams Industries, Cave Shepherd and Co. Ltd., and First Caribbean International Bank. I was grateful for this level of support, which brought the excitement of the ICCC into Barbadian homes.

In association with Saffire Productions, we chose Independence Day deliberately for these programmes because we knew that Barbadians would be looking forward to seeing something positive about nation-building on that day. I am sure that we did not disappoint them.

We also created a magazine called "The Blue Beret" to generate publicity. Produced on my computer, "The Blue Beret" provided information about what was happening in the Corps. The title arose out of a situation where some Cadet Corps officers were wondering why they could not wear the green beret of the Regular Force and the Regiment. Through the imagery, I sought to remind everyone of the value of the blue berets. I do not know if I was successful in getting that message across, but the magazine was successful in terms of keeping people informed about developments within the Corps.

The Barbados Cadet Corps became known to the Caribbean region through programmes like "Cadet Boot Camp" and a video featuring the 2005 camps in St. Lucia and St. Vincent, which were featured on Caribvision. The Barbados Cadet Corps became known to the world through its website, developed in 2006 by Lt. Col. Trevor Browne, Commandant, who was also web manager. News of all the action and exciting events was now available for cadets, parents, guardians, supporters and, indeed, international cadet corps to see what we were doing in Barbados.

In 2011, there was a massive publicity campaign targeting parents and guardians at the Lloyd Erskine Sandiford Centre. The room was filled with about twelve hundred people, including about five hundred cadets and seven hundred parents!

This was a deliberate attempt to publicize the Corps. I believe that during my tenure, many parents began to understand exactly what cadet training could do for their children and many opted to send them. The yearly recruiting programme involved as many as 350 children. This was due to the sensitization programmes and the return of cadet activities to the curricula in some of the schools.

23

The Value of Learning Languages

One aspect of my service to the Barbados Defence Force, as Staff Officer Cadets, which is lesser known or, perhaps forgotten, was my support as an interpreter in French and Spanish.

When I started full-time at the Barbados Cadet Corps Headquarters, I thought I would be leaving foreign languages behind. Although I knew that I would meet Spanish and French speaking people, I was not expecting to use the languages very much in my job. However, Chief of Staff, Brigadier Rudyard Lewis recognized that this was an area in which I could help the BDF.

On more than one occasion, I served as interpreter for the Defence Force. I recall that in 1996, when the SINSEC Conference was held in Barbados, involving security leaders from the Caribbean, the keynote speaker was a General from the Dominican Republic. I was his interpreter.

In the early days, when there were guests at formal dinners in the BDF Officers' Mess, I did spontaneous interpreting for both French and Spanish military personnel. Without a script to consult beforehand, I had to translate on the spot, which was both challenging and exciting.

The most special of these assignments was at Independence time in 1998 when I was attached to a French General who was on an official visit to Barbados. I was on the tarmac with Brigadier Lewis, and when he alighted from his helicopter. I translated Brigadier Lewis' greeting, "Good morning" ("Bonjour") and "Welcome to Barbados" ("Bienvenue à la Barbade") and the various sentiments expressed by the two parties throughout the journey to the various destinations.

I accompanied the same General to Government Headquarters and then to Government House, where we had lunch with the Governor-General. I sat at the table as an interpreter. Who would have thought that my language skills would lead me to such a point in life?

One year, at Independence time, when personnel from the Venezuela Army came to Barbados, I was selected as an interpreter for the group. There was to be a fly past during the ceremony involving their aircraft. I attended the planning meetings/briefings to interpret, take care of our guests, and ensure that everything ran smoothly from their perspective. I was also requested by Brigadier Lewis, from time to time, to interpret for him at functions in the BDF Officers' Mess involving Spanish and French military personnel.

Learning languages and using them broadens one's contacts and breaks down barriers of communication. There are not many people with this skill in Barbados, so it could be a very rewarding field for those who take the time to learn languages. For years, I taught my students the value of learning a language and, as it so happened, I was not only able to teach it, I was able to use it to help my country.

24

Commandants

As Staff Officer Cadets, I was responsible for the day-to-day management of the Cadet Headquarters, working alongside and in support of four Commandants – Lt. Col. Owen Springer, Lt. Col. Ron Clarke, Lt. Col. Neville Edwards and Lt. Col. Trevor Browne.

Commandants normally serve a period of three years before they are rotated.

Each Commandant had his own distinctive style and area of interest, but all were interested in the development of the Corps.

Lieutenant Colonel Springer brought his experience from the world of business to the Cadet Corps and his involvement in the military and scouting underpinned the decisions he made about the cadets. His wisdom earned him the respect of officers and cadets alike.

As a school Deputy Principal and former cadet leader, Lieutenant Colonel Clarke understood the fundamental child-related problems which we faced, and was able to bring his experience to bear on matters related to both adults and cadets.

In 2000, Lt. Col. Edwards went further, looking at strategic planning. He met with officers at an all-day seminar at St. James Secondary School and they developed the plan. Principals, cadets at various levels, former cadets, parents and other stakeholders were also consulted.

The result was a strategic plan for 2001 to 2011. We resolved to increase the number of cadets in the corps; establish a cadet advisory committee; seek greater autonomy for the Cadet Commandant; establish clearly defined terms and conditions of service for the Cadet Executive Officer; regularize the status of officers; improve the training available to cadets and adult leaders; design a webpage and newsletter; develop a network for linkages with other local and international youth organizations; and solicit sponsors for special projects.

In 2003, Lieutenant Colonel Edwards was appointed Permanent Secretary Defence and Security, and relinquished the post of Commandant. Lieutenant Colonel Trevor Browne became Acting Commandant, and was appointed Commandant in 2004.

In doing so, he became the first Commandant who had served solely as a Cadet Officer. All previous commandants were either officers in the Volunteer Force of the early years, the Barbados Regiment or the Barbados Defence Force. Would this usher in a new era of "cadetting" in Barbados?

25

A New and Exciting Era

Everything that we had accomplished so far faded in comparison with what we were able to achieve when Lieutenant Colonel Trevor Browne and I started working together. When I was a cadet, he was Sergeant Major. My respect for his personality and capabilities was long-standing.

Lieutenant Colonel Trevor Browne SCM.

Lieutenant Colonel Bowne first looked at the strategic goal of increasing the number of cadets to 2,500. He felt that, at a time when so many young people were going astray, the Cadet Corps could not be satisfied to provide training for only 1,000 students when there were about 24,000 to 27,000 children in the school system.

He felt that increased numbers could be achieved partly through the development of new units. He stressed the need for the separation of the band and sea cadet units and the development of a shooting programme and medical, police and sports units. He was sure that these would create interest and excitement.

Part-time Sea cadets in the early days at HMBS WILLOUGHBY FORT.

Full-time sea cadets at training.

Cadets of the shooting programme at Waterford Shooting range.

By separating the sea and band units, we eliminated the conflicts of interest which arose when school-based activities divided their loyalties. These conflicts of interest resulted in low attendance, and the separation allowed for growth.

Furthermore, these units would naturally attract people with particular interests in band and sea activities. This was a distinct change to the status quo. For almost one hundred years, the Barbados Cadet Corps was strongly based on the infantry type model. Hence, it was easy and more comfortable to keep that model.

The Sea Cadet Programme began to flourish under the command of Lt. Cdr. Carl Farley and later, Sub-Lieutenant Robert Morris.

Change always creates challenges for people who prefer to adhere to what they have always done. Lt. Col. Browne's answer to that was, "If we always do what we have always done, we will always get what we always got." He felt that we needed a paradigm shift, and so did we.

The next step in the plan was the establishment of a Medical Unit and a Shooting Programme. The Medical Unit, which was developed by Major Dennis Browne, himself a former medic, was tied to the medical unit at the BDF.

The Shooting Programme gained support from the shooting club at Waterford. This effort was also driven by Lt. Col.Trevor Browne, who was a member of the club.

Lt. Col Browne developed a cadet sports programme, and helped stage the first ever sports camp in Barbados. Instead of the normal training programme in map and compass, skill at arms, field craft and drill, this camp emphasized sports. Cadets were only required to bring sportswear to camp. It was exciting and a good addition to the year's programme.

Under Lt. Col. Neville Edwards, central recruiting added large numbers of recruits to the Corps. For example, in 1999, there were 350 new junior cadets in the annual parade reciting the cadet's pledge.

Junior cadets cleaning boots and hanging out clothes to dry.

Lt. Col. Browne maintained this focus on recruitment. Assisted by Major Peter Powlett and a group of dedicated officers, central recruiting was extended from just one term to a full year. Previously, when junior cadets graduated from central recruiting after one term of training, they often left their school unit soon afterwards. However, when they recruited for a full year, large numbers of junior cadets were still available for summer camp, the first of which was held in 2004 at the Paragon Base campsite. It was an excellent opportunity to develop the skills needed.

These initiatives had a positive impact on membership in the Cadet Corps. Within the ten-year period of the strategic development plan, there were 1,400 cadets on roll.

Athletes practicing dining etiquette.

We also provided training for the young potential athletes of the Barbados Olympic Association (BOA), with whom we worked to stage the inaugural training camp for potential olympic athletes. The event took place from December 16-23, 2006 at the Regional Police Training Centre (RPTC), Christ Church.

Potential Olympic athletes on an adventurous training exercise as part of a team-building programme conducted by the Barbados Cadet Corps.

The programme enhanced the spirit of camaraderie and teamwork among the potential olympic athletes and taught them basic survival skills. The programme also taught life skills; developed initiative; and exposed participants to practical training in etiquette, team-building and various aspects of the Olympic Games. Forty potential athletes participated in the first camp. The second camp, staged a year later, continued to show the flexibility of our training programme and its relevance to training outside the boundaries of the military setting. I have always felt that the Cadet Corps could provide team-building training for corporate Barbados. Young business professionals could take part in retreats and practical leadership training at our campsite. These sessions would allow management to learn more about their capabilities as leaders. Perhaps because of our busy overseas camp schedule and local training initiatives, we were never able to explore that possibility except when we were working with Parish Ambassadors and with the potential olympic athletes.

26

Local and Overseas Caribbean Camps

2003: Barbados Cadet Corps contingent to St. Lucia led by Capt. David Clarke and Lt. Rosalind Conliffe.

The real challenge in administration was handling several initiatives simultaneously, and with Lt. Col. Browne as Commandant, the Barbados Cadet Corps Headquarters was a hive of activity.

From 2003 onwards, we embarked on very ambitious arrangements for camps with our Caribbean neighbours. Since the early 1980s, we had attended all Caribbean camps when they were staged by St. Lucia, St. Vincent and the Organization of the Eastern Caribbean (OECS) States.

Caribbean Cadet Camps in Barbados

Although we had hosted Caribbean Cadet Camps in 1991 and 1997, I was uncomfortable with the idea that these events only catered for nineteen cadets per country annually. Yet, there were twenty-two units in the Barbados Cadet Corps. This meant that only one cadet per unit could travel, and at least three units would not be represented at all. Opportunities to attend overseas camps helped to keep the students excited and motivated. Under normal circumstances, there were cadets who might not have been able to travel on their family's budget. A cadet camp, however, allowed them to go overseas at minimum expense to them.

Therefore, we encouraged bilateral camps with Cadet Corps from neighbouring Caribbean countries, like St. Lucia in 2003.

Later, a link was established between the South Zone of the Barbados Cadet Corps and the battalion in the South of Trinidad. This resulted in a meaningful exchange arrangement. The then Major Trevor Browne who was South Zone Commander and Major Zeno Crepin, Commander of South Battalion of the Trinidad and Tobago Cadet Force and who eventually became Commandant of the Trinidad and Tobago Cadet Corps, collaborated to develop this exchange between the Barbados Cadet Corps and the Trinidad and Tobago Cadet Force. This exchange took place during Easter vacations.

When the Barbados Cadet Corps celebrated its 100th Anniversary in 2004, a Caribbean Camp was held in July/August to commemorate the occasion. Whereas the camp of 1997 was held under tents, by 2004, cadets were lodged in buildings on the campsite at the BDF base at Paragon.

One of the highlights of this camp was a Guard of Honour Ceremony for the Governor-General. This involved cadets from all the participating countries and the Barbados Cadet Corps band, augmented by members of the Dominica Cadet Corps band. The ceremony was held on the grounds of Government House, and the then Governor-General, His excellency Sir Clifford Husbands G.C.M.G., K.A, a former cadet, inspected the Guard of Honour. Afterwards, the cadets were granted the rare privilege of socializing in the garden at Government House.

The Commandants of the various cadet companies were present at this ceremony. They were attending the Commandants' Conference, which was held in the conference room of the Pommarine Hotel.

The Caribbean Cadet Commandants' Conferences were held in conjunction with these camps. The 1997 conference was held in the Central Liason Office of the Regional Security System and the camp was held at our campsite at Paragon. I had deliberately chosen that conference room for its round table, which allowed the delegates to feel that they had an equal say in matters being discussed, regardless of their rank.

In 2004, the Commandants witnessed the closing parade, which was held on the BDF parade square at Paragon. The parade was commanded by a schoolboy, Cadet Senior Under Officer Beckles, from the Princess Margaret Cadet Company. The reviewing officer was the Chief of Staff of the BDF, Colonel Alvin Quintyne.

St. Lucia Camp, 2005

From July 15 to 31, 2005, members of the Barbados Cadet Corps participated in camps in St. Lucia, Trinidad and St. Vincent. These camps were designed to motivate the cadets by providing opportunities to camp in large numbers overseas. They were also intended to allow Barbadian cadets to develop bonds of friendships with their counterparts in other Caribbean countries.

This camp in St Lucia - a Star 4 camp - was completed in two phases. Phase 1 was held in Barbados from July 11 to 15. When the recce was done in St. Lucia prior to the camp, it was agreed that the St. Lucian cadets would join the Barbadians for Phase 1 of training and then both units would go to St. Lucia for Phase 2. This was our way of ensuring that all Star 4 cadets participating in this training qualified for their badges having covered all aspects of the course.

Barbadian and St. Lucian Star 4 Cadets on their adventurous Training Exercise in St. Lucia.

As planned, cadets and an adult leader from the St. Lucia Cadet Corps traveled to Barbados on July 9 to attend Phase 1 and left Barbados on July 15 to attend Phase 2 in St. Lucia.

We took several precautionary measures to ensure the safety of everyone at camp. A recce was carried out by Capt. Errol Brathwaite, officer in charge of the Star 4 course, in June 2005 to plan the event in conjunction with the St. Lucian officers. Seven officers, including five males and two females accompanied the cadets on the hike in totally unfamiliar territory. There were two female officers in case one of them needed to leave with a female cadet to seek medical attention. A medic from the BDF, LCpl. Nurse A, also accompanied the group on the hike. In addition, arrangements were made with the St. Lucia Cadet Corps for some of its officers to travel on foot with the group. Capt. Dennis Browne from Cadet Headquarters was responsible for providing administrative assistance while the group was in St. Lucia.

Capt. Errol Brathwaite watches with pride as a Barbadian Cadet receives a certificate from St. Lucia's Governor-General

At the end of the camp, there was a Closing Ceremony at which St. Lucia's Governor-General, Dame Pearlette Louisy GCSL GCMG, presented the awards and certificates. Certificates were presented to both Barbadian and St. Lucian Cadets. It was pleasing to note that the cadet programme received support at the highest level in St. Lucia.

Eartha and author at Government House in St. Lucia with Capt. Cyril Saltibus, Aide-de-camp.

Earlier that year, while on a recce in St. Lucia, I had had the pleasure of meeting her at Government House when both my wife and I were invited by Commandant Major Andre Mathurin to pay a Courtesy Call on Dame Pearlette of the St. Lucia Cadet Corps. It was a truly memorable visit.

By all reports, both phases of the camp were successfully executed.

St. Vincent Camp, 2005

While the Star 4 cadets were in St. Lucia, back at home, Cadet Headquarters staff were handling administrative matters for local camp and preparing for the next group of cadets to travel to St. Vincent. This second mission involved sea cadets, cadet band members and a drill display team from the infantry cadets, who were due to leave just one week after the first group had departed for St. Lucia.

Flashback to the 1975 departure from the Baggage Wharehouse

On Friday, July 22, sea cadets left Barbados on board the Coast Guard ship, HMBS TRIDENT to commence exercise "Blue Wave." I was at the Coast Guard base, HMBS WILLOUGHBY FORT, when they boarded and left Barbados at 2130 hours. Lt. Cdr. Farley, PCO Tyrone Edwards and twenty sea cadets stood majestically on deck dressed in their uniforms and life vests, as their parents waved goodbye.

Cdr. Dave Dowridge, the then Deputy Chief of Staff of the BDF, was standing near to me. We both recalled that time, thirty years before, when we were both leaving Barbados on the SEIMSTRAND from this very location which had a different name. It was the Baggage Wharehouse then. We were also destined for St. Vincent. This was a joint effort of all three existing cadet companies in one of the rare activities where units merged. For the greater part of the year, individual units generally proceeded with their own activities and only came together for ceremonial parades, sports and summer camps. Even then they paraded as separate detachments with their own officers in command and, during camps, they trained in separate platoons or companies. What I was witnessing now with children from many different schools fully integrated showed me the progress we had made in terms of building the social fabric over the past thirty years. I was happy to have played a part in this arrangement, where young Barbadian cadets could have a similar experience.

These cadets were preceded by an advance party of adults, including Capt. Sandra Norville, Lt. Delisle Bascombe and WO2 Cherrol Deane.

The following day, Saturday, July 23, members of the Cadet Band and infantry left Barbados in groups on Caribbean Star airlines, and by 1800 hours, all personnel of the Cadet Corps were accounted for in St Vincent.

I also travelled to St. Vincent and had the pleasure of witnessing all of the activities done by the cadets.

In keeping with the traditional format for camps dating back to 1975, we included vital support services. The medic, Lt. Cpl. Nurse, of the BDF was assisted by Ms. Mary Thompson, a nurse from The Barbados Light and Power Co. Ltd., who volunteered her services. We were happy to have her because of the number of female cadets in the camp.

Meals were provided by a catering group comprising three adults (Lt. Delisle Bascombe, Lt. Naomi Williams and Sgt. Patricia Marshall of the BDF) and three female cadets (L/Cpl. Lynette Lynch (No. 19 Unit – Deighton Griffith), Cdt. Kemeisha Marshall and Cdt. Tiffany Joseph (No. 9 – Parkinson Memorial), who were very keen on Home Economics. This was the birth of our catering unit.

Displays were held in Heritage Square in Kingstown, Calliaqua and Campden Park, where people congregated for social activities. Intense morning rehearsals resulted in outstanding performances by the band, drill squad and sea cadets, who were true ambassadors for Barbados. Many officers and cadets of the St. Vincent and the Grenadines Cadet Force marveled at the displays on each occasion.

The Barbadian sea cadets were delighted to share their experiences with a small detachment of sea cadets from St. Vincent. They also enjoyed a number of water-based activities against the backdrop of Young Island and a location near Blue Lagoon.

A film crew from Saffire Productions arrived on the 24th and departed on the 26th July after recording the display and the sea cadets' activities.

I was invited to participate in a one-hour radio interview on Cross-Country Radio with the Commandant of St. Vincent and the Grenadines Cadet Force. I also took part in a television interview which was aired on the 27th during the St. Vincent television evening news. Both interviews dealt with the strong relationship between both Corps and the importance of "cadetting" to the region.

The Commandant of the Cadet Corps, Lt. Col. Trevor Browne, used his own resources to visit St. Vincent and St. Lucia, and spent two days at each camp location. His presence reassured the officers and cadets of both local and overseas units of his interest and commitment.

These camps in St Vincent and St Lucia were highly successful. Previously, only ten to nineteen cadets would have attended camp overseas, but this new arrangement saw approximately 154 cadets traveling overseas all in one month. This move was a tremendous motivator for both adults and cadets. We had achieved our objective to have a safe and enjoyable overseas camp experience, and in the process, we created a blueprint for future overseas camps.

After the Star 4 camp in St Lucia, we agreed that it would be useful to alternate this activity among Caribbean countries with similar terrain. Dominica was chosen, and it became an important destination for future Star 4 adventurous training exercises.

Overseas Camps in 2006

In 2006, we raised the bar higher, staging camps simultaneously in four territories, all under the supervision of a team of officers and permanent staff instructors. Star 2 and 3 cadets camped in St. Lucia with over 150 attendees. Sea cadets went to Antigua; a shooting team to Jamaica and Star 4 cadets journeyed to Dominica for their adventurous training exercise. This was a true indication of how much the Corps had developed. Progress was possible through selfless contributions from officers; parents; guardians; principals; and personnel from the Barbados Defence Force. Cadets themselves raised much of the funds needed to cover travel costs.

Sea Cadets depart for Antigua on board HMBS TRIDENT

Sea Cadets Visit Antigua

SLt. Robert Morris was Contingent Commander of the fifty sea cadets who set out for Antigua to experience their second summer camp. On July 20, 2006, HMBS TRIDENT departed Barbados for Antigua around 1015 hours with twenty-five cadets on board under the supervision of SLt. R. Morris and ASL Petra Sealy. Their mission was to integrate with the new sea unit of the Antigua and Barbuda National Cadet Corps and assist them by sharing experiences and training. Throughout the exercises, they were accompanied by Coast Guard personnel to ensure their safety and high standards of training.

The remaining cadets left Barbados by air on July 21. A BDF cook Pte. David Inniss provided the meals.

The sea cadets returned to Barbados at 1900 hours on July 31, while those who traveled by air departed Antigua on July 30.

Visit to St. Lucia

Major Peter Powlett served as Camp Commandant when Star 2, Star 3 and band cadets traveled to St Lucia for their summer camp. The camp was held just outside Castries at the Castries Secondary School. Cadets from the St. Lucia Cadet Corps also attended the camp and did everything possible to ensure the comfort of their guests and the smooth running of the event.

The high points of the camp were the organized recreational activities which showed the great team spirit which existed among members of the Corps. The first four days were spent preparing for a hike, which was ultimately called off because of severe water outages and heavy rains which flooded the kitchen. This was a difficult time, and conditions were potentially hazardous and unsanitary. We made do with boiled and bottled water, and were determined to function within the imposed limitations. However, we decided to return to Barbados when, several days after the initial outage, the authorities were unable to say definitively when the water would be restored.

Booking flights for 150 people on LIAT planes, with limited seating, was a tremendous task, especially since we were changing the original flight dates. Nevertheless, we worked with personnel at the LIAT office and our flights were confirmed for July 30 and 31. This was a testing time for me and, by far, one of my greatest challenges.

Cadets get ready to board the bus for their tour of Dominica.

Star 4 Cadet Camp in Dominica

While we were grappling with the problem in St. Lucia, Captain David Clarke, Contingent Leader and Camp Commandant for the elite Star 4 group, was blissfully unaware of our challenges. He, his officers and cadets were participating in the adventurous training camp in Dominica, and were about to tackle Dominica's highest mountain, Mont Diablotin. Twenty-five senior cadets from Dominica joined our twenty cadets for this phase.

The camp was held in Portsmouth at the Portsmouth Secondary School, and support from the Dominica Cadet Corps was outstanding. In fact, we benefitted from the cooperation and support of everyone from the level of the Commandant, Major Richards, to the officers, cadets, members of the police force and the residents of Dominica. Prime Minister Roosevelt Skerrit himself paid an informal visit and said a few words of encouragement to the cadets.

Lt. Col. Trevor Browne (right) with Star 4 cadets in Dominica.

Our Star 4 cadets were fascinated by the vegetation and ruggedly different terrain of Dominica, through which they hiked, arriving at the highest point on the island at an elevation of 4,747 feet.

A tour of the island included stops at some of the most remarkable natural wonders, including the Freshwater Lake at 3000 feet up in the clouds, the twin waterfalls and the city of Roseau. The experience which stands out in their minds, however, remains the vehicular exploits of Dominican drivers.

The Cadet Commandant, Lt. Col. Trevor Browne, visited the camps in St. Lucia and Dominica, at his own expense, as he had done in 2005. As usual, his presence lifted everyone's spirits and served as a good public relations opportunity. In St Lucia, he was a great help during the water crisis, helping to clear the lines of the water tank situated on the roof of the building in which the camp was taking place. His problem solving skills were reminiscent of former commandants such as Lt. Col. R. Clarke, who attended camps and spent a great deal of time helping to make the campsite as functional as possible.

Barbados Cadet Corps shooting team in Jamaica.

Jamaica

Captain Errol Brathwaite, PCO Emmanuel Ward and eight cadets set off for Jamaica on July 19, 2006 to attend the Caribbean Cadet Camp. Their mission was to participate fully in the camp and represent Barbados in the Caribbean Cadet Shooting Competition. They placed fifth, as was reported by Capt. Brathwaite.

Star 4 Camp in Tobago

Reference has already been made to the camps involving Barbadian and Canadian cadets between 2006 and 2010. In 2007, there was an International Cadet Challenge Camp which will be the subject of the entire next chapter in these memoirs. In 2008, the Caribbean Camp was held in St. Vincent and the Grenadines and, in 2010, Trinidad and Tobago staged the camp as part of their centenary celebrations. The Barbados Cadet Corps participated in all these events.

By 2011, the number of Star 4 cadets had increased. The annual Star 4 expedition was held in Tobago from Tuesday, July 19 to Monday, July 25 of that year. The camp was based at the Roxborough Secondary School, located near a rain forest and surrounded by hills.

An advance party comprising the Contingent Commander, Capt. S. Norville; the Permanent Staff Instructor, Sgt. Boyce S; and the cook, Pte. Vaughn S left Barbados on July 17.

The officers on this trip were Capt. Sandra Norville as Contingent Commander, Lt. Philip Eno, 2Lt. Ward, 2Lt. Desmond Grant, 2Lt. Rita Evans, 2Lt. Marcella Holford and PCO Geoffrey Wallace. The Permanent Staff Instructor from the BDF was Sgt. Samuel Boyce, who was a member of Cadet Headquarters staff and a very impressive instructor, who played a key role in this camp. Pte. Maycock H and Pte. Vaughn S served as the medic and cook respectively.

Capt. Norville mentioned in her report that, there were also eleven members of the Trinidad and Tobago Cadet Force attached to the camp: four on course and seven attached to messing.

She also noted that the main activities were the orienteering, the physical training exercises, the church service and the drill displays.

Training sessions were arranged in preparation for the orienteering competition. Route cards were drawn up and a run along a trail took place in the district surrounding the Roxborough Secondary School. For the competition, groups of cadets were expected to locate a number of points in Friendsfield (close to Scarborough), within a specified time frame.

A church service also aided our public relations effort. Members of the Trinidad and Tobago Cadet Force, the Commandant and other officers joined our cadets who participated in the service. Conducted by a husband and wife team and an instrumentalist, the service was held at a small Baptist church. Afterwards, the cadets marched back to the camp site.

The cadets also made full use of the opportunity to enhance their shooting skills, with a contest at Forte Cambleton. However, they first had to hike a short distance to the range, where they used .22 caliber rifles.

Besides the usual daily exercises, the cadets participated in a two-mile run during one of the training sessions conducted by 2Lt. D. Grant. The training was intense, and required the cadets to climb one of the hills surrounding the school. The recreational sessions were designed not only to test the stamina of the cadets, but to build team spirit and assess their ability to accomplish simple tasks under unfamiliar and trying conditions.

Similarly, the displays were meant to showcase the talents of the contingent and to publicize the Barbados Cadet Corps. In preparation for the event, a number of practice sessions were held, both prior to, and on arrival at the camp site. Members of the Trinidad and Tobago Cadet Force participated during the in-camp sessions. Two of them were selected to be part of the squad for the display, which included a series of precision drill movements, both with and without arms.

The second display, filmed by the Channel 5 Radio and Television Station, was held at the Port and was witnessed by passengers disembarking from the T&T Express. CSM Beckles did a remarkable job and the detachment received glowing compliments from the ship's captain, who saw the entire demonstration.

Detailed planning

Before any of these camps could take place, it was necessary to conduct recces in the proposed territories. Recces determined what needed to be done to guarantee a successful event.

Over the years, I developed a checklist for planning camps, which was used on recces. The checklist highlighted the administrative requirements and reduced the possibility of forgetting important details. We checked on the availability of beds/cots and how these would be transported. There was also the matter of toilet and bath facilities, and decisions as to whether field showers were to be erected. Lighting and security fencing were also important items on the checklist. With regard to safety, we always worked with someone with local knowledge to help plan the routes and identify any potential safety issues. The risk analysis was very important. We were always conscious of our responsibility to the authorities and to parents and guardians to ensure a pleasant and safe camping experience.

We also developed a system for funding the camps, where Cadet Corps Public Funds, the schools of participating cadets, and parents or guardians each paid one third of the cost. This formula worked very well, and there were a few occasions when the cadets were able to raise all the money for the airfare themselves.

We achieved great success in conceptualizing, planning, and managing these overseas camps. However, there was one event which came to represent the epitome of success. It was the International Cadet Challenge Camp (ICCC) - the ultimate camp experience!

27

International Cadet Challenge Camp – An Ingenious Plan

The Victorious Barbados Cadet Corps Team.

The overseas camps were thrilling and required a great deal of administrative work by the Barbados Cadet Corps Headquarters. But in my opinion, the greatest effort was put into organizing the International Cadet Challenge Camp, conceptualized by Lt. Col Trevor Browne.

Lt. Col. Browne felt that our Corps needed to benchmark its standards against those of the rest of the "cadetting" world. This was part of our new approach to cadet training. Previously, training in summer camps was interspersed with competitions, tours, lectures and exams. The International

Obstacle course.

Cadet Challenge Camp was totally different. All the military skills learnt were used in an intense competition, where teams fielded the best cadets in their ranks.

The ICCC included an obstacle course, a triathlon, a team relay race and competitions in public speaking, drill, orienteering, shooting and survival techniques. The ICCC involved eight days of intense competition, during which time we witnessed the ecstasy of victory and the agony of defeat as team fortunes fluctuated.

Issued with special colour-coded shirts, compliments the Barbados Cadet Corps, the contingents were easily identified when not in uniform. Also, each participant had a special name tag bearing his/her photo.

The two days before the start of the competition were dedicated to rotational training in preparation for the obstacle course, weapons, equipment, and drill sequences.

Obstacle Course

The competition began early on the morning of the third day, pitting the teams in a grueling obstacle challenge. Participants jumped over water; crawled under barbed wire; scaled six to twelve-foot walls; and literally conquered the highs and lows of other obstacles.

All team members had to finish together and, in some cases, it was necessary for the stronger cadets to assist their weaker comrades who had fallen, and urge them to press on to the finish line.

St. Vincent and the Grenadines made a dramatic start to the games, winning this first event in the inaugural ICCC.

Swimming aspect of Triathlon

Contestants cycling.

Barbadian cadet wins Team Triathlon.

Triathlon

My favourite event in the competition was the triathlon. Contestants were required to swim a distance of fifty meters to a marker in the sea, then turn and swim back to shore. Each contestant wore a life vest, and the Barbados Coast Guard provided a safety boat and personnel.

On exiting the water, they mounted bicycles and rode off on a predetermined route to the start of a foot race to the finish line. This was a fast-paced and very keenly contested event, which was expertly managed by the Barbados Triathlon Association.

It was a real test of physical endurance, and an activity never before done in the long history of the Barbados Cadet Corps.

Drill Competition

During the drill competition, I felt very proud of the Barbados team. Their turnout was immaculate and they marched with a precision which I had not seen before in my almost forty years of association with the Cadet Corps. Lieutenant Michael Boyce, who led this team, was succeeded by Capt. Errol Brathwaite in 2009 and 2011. Both men did an excellent job in motivating the cadets.

Winner of the Drill Challenge Barbados Cadet Corps Team.

Cadets in the field enjoying a meal.

Orienteering

Survival and Orienteering Challenges

Orienteering and survival training were all part of a major field exercise set against the backdrop of the picturesque East Coast of Barbados, where cadets set up harbours, built shelters and prepared meals.

Command tasks tested the military knowledge and skills of the teams, which were scored on leadership, discipline, planning, execution, creativity and security over a 24-hour period.

The orienteering competition was conducted during the survival training aspect of the event. There was a common start and finish point, from which each team departed at five-minute intervals. Twelve target event locations were marked on the map and identified on the ground. Each target had an allocated value ranging from five to twenty points.

Contestants, working in teams, were given a number of grid references (locations on the map). Each location carried a score. The points which were furthest away from the bivouac area were given a higher value than those which were closer. Teams could not possibly get to all the locations in the time allotted, so they had to plan carefully to determine which ones they would attempt to reach.

Shooting Competition

Full bore weapons were used for the shooting competition, which was supervised by Captain Errol Brathwaite. Captain Brathwaite, the only Corps officer authorized to run a full bore range at the time, served as Range Officer. Cadets relished the idea of shooting

Captian Errol Brathwaite

Winner of the Shooting Competition

Winner of the Commandants Challenge

Judges

these weapons, and after completing the requisite practice sessions, the BDF allowed them to take part in the event. Captain Brathwaite was assisted by Colour Sergeant Knight and a team of safety personnel from the BDF.

In the 2009 and 2011 competition, Lt. Col. Browne made a rack with falling plates of different sizes and point values. Teams were required to demonstrate their marksmanship skills by shooting down the plates as quickly as possible, using the least amount of pellets.

Commandant's Challenge

The flagship event was the Commandant's Challenge, in which teams executed a number of military exercises, using cadet training in field craft, skill-at-arms, and tactics. Teams were issued with electronic laser weapons and mission instructions thirty minutes before the start. The challenge sought to test the physical fitness, team spirit, resourcefulness and technical and leadership skills of the participants in knock-out rounds.

Winner of Speak Off Dominica Cadet Corps

Public Speaking Competition

The Public Speaking competition, also known as the Youth Forum, provided practical experience in the fundamental skills of public speaking and offered a platform for cadets from other nations and backgrounds to present their views on selected topics.

As I listened to the concerns of the young people, I noted that we all shared the same challenges within the region. The Chief Judge was Mr. Victor Hutchinson, a former Principal of Parkinson Secondary School. Major Andy White of the Cayman Islands also served as a judge.

This type of activity was hardly ever done at summer camps in the region, which accounts for its novelty and impact.

Tug O' War Competition.

Adult officers' turn to participate.

Sports Challenge

The sports challenge tested the cadets' ability to compete in a number of physical and mental challenges in a competitive but friendly atmosphere. The sports day began with an opening ceremony and a parade of teams. Events were announced at specific intervals, and contestants moved to the starting line for traditional athletic events and races of all kinds, including relays and racquet and sack races.

The tug o' war created a lot of excitement, as teams battled to show their strength and superiority. However, it was not just fun and games for the cadets. There were a few events for the adults, among which were the roller races, using the metal part of a bicycle wheel controlled with a stick. These races were popular when I was a little boy, and participants who may have had similar childhood experiences showed their skills in maneuvering the rollers. It was a hilarious and enjoyable spectacle.

Relay Races

Teams for the relay races comprised six cadets, of whom a minimum of two were girls and one under sixteen years old. They were required to complete the race (approximately 6 km) with runners stationed at fixed points along the route. The team could only win when every member had crossed the finish line in the shortest time possible. Relay races always generate a lot of interest and this was no exception.

Social and Cultural Activity

The competition continued daily, breaking only for an island tour on "Kadooment Day," when they witnessed the revelry and enjoyed the carnival atmosphere.

Cadets lower the flags of their countries

A Solemn Moment

At the end of each day, the flags of the participating countries were lowered. This was a solemn ceremony, at which the retreat was sounded by a bugler from the Cadet Band. Two cadets representing each country were responsible for lowering the flags and taking them to a room to be secured.

The Trinidad and Tobago Cadet Force won the 2007 competition, with Barbados coming in second. The battle between these two teams reminded me of the traditional clashes between Barbados and Trinidad in a number of other sporting arenas.

Trinidad and Tobago Cadet Force wins the 2007 ICCC

The Barbados Cadet Corps receiving the second place award from the Attorney-General, the Hon. Dale Marshall, (2007)

Barbados and Nottinghamshire ACF share the trophy for 1st place, (2009)

The awards ceremony was held at the prestigious Frank Collymore Hall, where the Hon. Dale Marshall, Attorney-General, delivered the feature address and presented the prizes. Captain John Morodore did an excellent job as Master of Ceremonies.

This loss to Trinidad gave the Barbados Cadet Corps team an even greater incentive to win the competition in 2009.

I was pleased with the outstanding effort of the Barbados team whenever the competitions were held. They performed extremely well, showing that they were a well-synchronized team with strong military skills.

The organizers were pleased with the results of the ICCC. A cadet from one of the countries represented, described it as "the greatest development in cadetting history."

This was a great honour for the Barbados Cadet Corps.Nottinghamshire Army Cadet Force from the United Kingdom joined the competition for the first time in 2009 and tied with the Barbados Cadet Corps for first place.

It required a great deal of skill to stage this activity. Having attended many international tournaments, our Commandant presided over this event with confidence and with the type of efficiency which made him respected by participants from the various countries.

Lt. Col. Browne knew that he could rely on me to handle the administration for this massive undertaking, and was confident in the ability of his keen and dedicated officers to assist with planning. Although officers, who were working in jobs outside Cadet Headquarters, planned certain aspects of the event, Cadet Headquarters was ultimately responsible for coordinating the support effort and ensuring that all systems were in place. It meant notifying overseas participants and working out the details of the budgets for 2007, 2009 and 2011.

Teams of cadets from Trinidad and Tobago, the Cayman Islands, St. Vincent and the Grenadines, Dominica, Grenada and the British Virgin Islands participated in the competition. In 2009 and 2011, they were joined by teams from Nottinghamshire Army Cadet Force.

The presentation ceremony came in the final phase of planning. The ceremonies for the first two competitions took place at the Frank Collymore Hall and we invited a minister of government to present the awards, in keeping with our decision to maintain high standards.

The media was also invited to cover the story and, by the following day, it was on television and in the local press.

Sample of teams represented at ICCC

I am glad that I was able to experience this competition. It reminded me that, with some creativity, it was possible to take the training of our youths to a higher level. We had previously used the slogan "A Stitch in Time Saves Nine," to stress the urgent need to capture the interest of our young people. Now, we were acting on our new slogan: "Boldly Going Where No One Has Gone Before."

Cadet Corps personnel seated in the Frank Collymore Hall.

28

Assistance to Cayman Islands and Tortola.

Author with Mr. Roy Bodden (extreme left) and family on one of his trips to Barbados.

Cayman Islands

The news on the Barbados Cadet Corps' website spread and two countries started to look at how Barbados could assist them. The first of these was the Cayman Islands, whose Minister of Tourism and Minister of Education came to Barbados on a mission to learn more about certain aspects of the island which they admired. The Minister of Education was Hon. Roy Bodden. He selected the Barbados Cadet Corps and requested a meeting with me at Cadet Headquarters, where I explained our training philosophy and the way the system worked.

Lt. Col. Bobeth O'Garro Commandant, Cayman Islands Cadet Corps.

They subsequently sent two potential leaders from the police force to take part in an orientation exercise and familiarization tour. The Barbados Cadet Corps was staging a camp at the same time. This allowed the visitors to observe the training and how our system functioned. One of these visitors was Mr. Philip Hyre, who eventually became Commandant.

He was also one of the first two officers to be trained on the Potential Cadet Officers Course in Barbados. The other officer was Mrs. Bobeth O'Garro, now a Lieutenant Colonel, who is currently Commandant of the Cayman Islands Cadet Corps.

By 2002, a unit was firmly established in the Cayman Islands. Mr. Hyre became the first Commandant at the rank of Lieutenant Colonel and Mrs. O'Garro became the first Cadet Executive Officer in the rank of Major. She has become a very good friend of mine.

Since then, other officers from the Cayman Islands Cadet Corps have come to Barbados to attend the Potential Cadet Officers Training Course. The Cayman Islands Cadet Corps is also a strong supporter of our International Cadet Challenge Camp.

Mr. Roy Bodden also became a good friend of mine, and would invite my wife and me to lunch whenever he came to Barbados. This was, for him, duty beyond the desk.

Capt. Selwyn Rock.

Tortola

In 2009, a request came from Tortola, British Virgin Islands for me to help them establish a Cadet Corps. The request was initiated by two former cadets; Sergeants Selwyn Rock and Rawle Gibbons, both members of the Royal Virgin Islands Police Force. They said they remembered the impact I had on their lives and wanted the same for the children of Tortola. Captain Rock became the first Cadet Commandant of this new unit and Captain Gibbons was the first Cadet Executive Officer. I was given special leave to visit Tortola for one week, as their government had agreed to cover my expenses.

Capt. Rawle Gibbons.

My wife Eartha accompanied me as she had on most of my overseas trips. We paid the additional airfare and she was able to share in my experiences.

On arrival at the airport, we were greeted on the tarmac with a welcome sign and taken to the VIP lounge. I had been briefed that a number of courtesy calls had been set up and would begin with a visit to the Governor's office. Following this, I would meet with the Premier, the Hon. Ralph O'Neale, followed by the Deputy Premier and then the members of the cabinet. These courtesy calls were held daily and I enjoyed sharing the value of cadet training and explaining how the system worked.

After the visits to government officials, attention was turned to Principals of secondary schools in Tortola and Virgin Gorda. I met with the Principals of North Sound Primary Schools and Bregado Flax Educational Center. My final obligation was an address to a luncheon held by the Rotary Club – a potential source of financing for the soon to be established Virgin Islands Cadet Corps.

Commissioner Reynell Frazier presenting me with a plaque.

I was humbled by a special mid-week reception in my honour at Government House. The Governor, ministers of government and other influential people attended.

The Commissioner of Police, Mr. Frazier, invited my wife and me to a music concert. He also presented me with a plaque in his office, in appreciation of my support.

We had the honour of having lunch with the Minister of Education and, also, at the residence of the Hon. Vernon Malone, former Police Commissioner and a strong supporter of the Cadet Corps – gestures which we really appreciated.

Mission Tortola

I was pleased to note that immediately after my visit to Tortola, the Virgin Islands Cadet Corps (VICC) was established. To support this effort. I conceptualized a mission for Barbadian cadets to go to Tortola to train the new cadets,

Star 4 level cadets in Barbados were required to travel overseas to do their adventurous training exercise, and Tortola and Virgin Gorda offered the perfect opportunity for the Barbadian cadet instructors to practice their craft.

A contingent of twenty-three cadets participated in this exercise under the supervision of three adult officers – Lieutenants Philip Eno, Michael Boyce and Erma Holder, from July 16 to 23, 2009. Our contingent received an extremely gracious welcome by everyone in the British Virgin Islands, and a reception in their honour was held at the campsite.

As part of a publicity campaign, the Star 4 cadets conducted three route marches to draw the public's attention to the cadet corps.

During their field training exercise, the cadets explored parts of Tortola and then travelled by boat to Virgin Gorda, another island in the Virgin Islands chain, to continue their expedition. They hiked to Baths National Park, explored caves and other places of interest. While in Tortola, they journeyed to the highest point on the island - Sage Mountain.

From all reports, the training provided by the star cadets was of great help to the VICC, whose members were inspired by the Barbadians.

My visit to Tortola and my involvement in assisting the Cayman Islands and the developments which occurred thereafter are special events in my life. They showed me that what we had been doing for more than a century meant something to a new "cadetting" fraternity. I am pleased to have helped establish two new corps in one decade.

I had also been involved in helping to revive and sustain growth in other Caribbean cadet corps / forces.

29

Assistance to Dominica Cadet Corps

WO 2 Cherrol Deane training Potential Officers of the Dominica Cadet Corps at Castle Bruce, Dominica.

Students in the classroom.

The Dominica Cadet Corps started in the early 1900s. But when the then Captain Francis Richards visited me, the unit was dormant, and he was progressing in his effort to rebuild it. Based on the goodwill shown by Dominicans towards us at Camp Londonderry in 1974, I felt that I needed to do my best to help, and gladly provided him with training materials.

In 2004, when we were celebrating the 100th Anniversary of the Barbados Cadet Corps, we staged the Caribbean camp in Barbados. Assisted by Cdr. Wilbert Kirton, we worked on an initiative to bring a contingent of cadets and their leaders from Dominica to the camp. The British High Commission and ALICO were involved in providing funding. This funding also made it possible for the Commandant, Major Richards, to attend the Commandants' Conference in Barbados.

Three years later, in 2007, there was a need to train adults, as the Dominica Cadet Corps was expanding. During the Easter vacation of that year, a team of officers and Permanent Staff Instructors from the Barbados Cadet Corps Headquarters, ably led by Capt. Dennis Browne, journeyed to Dominica to conduct a train-the-trainers' programme at Castle Bruce. The group included other experienced staffers from the BDF Cadet Headquarters: namely, WO 2 Cherrol Deane and Sgt. Gregory Broomes, both of whom brought their knowledge and passion for "cadetting" to bear as they trained the adult officers of the Dominica Cadet Corps.

This programme was funded by the United Nations Development Programme (UNDP).

The enthusiasm of the students on the course motivated the trainers. Training large numbers of personnel was an essential process in providing supervision and training for a Corps which was increasing. We were happy to assist in such a tangible way, and were pleased that the UNDP caught our vision to help our Caribbean neighbours.

With Major Francis Richards and his wife Daphne

I took vacation during that period and travelled with my wife to Dominica as guests of Major Richards and his wife Daphne. I had first met Major Francis Richards in Barbados when he came to Cadet Headquarters seeking information for a revival of the Dominica Cadets Corps. It was then I discovered that he was one of the cadets who was in our camp in Dominica in 1974. Even then, I was impressed by his commitment.

I was also impressed with the efficient way in which Capt. Dorsen Robin communicated. He too had previously visited Barbados and had taken the time to make contact with me to seek assistance. As a result of his excellent work in support of this training activity, administrative arrangements ran smoothly.

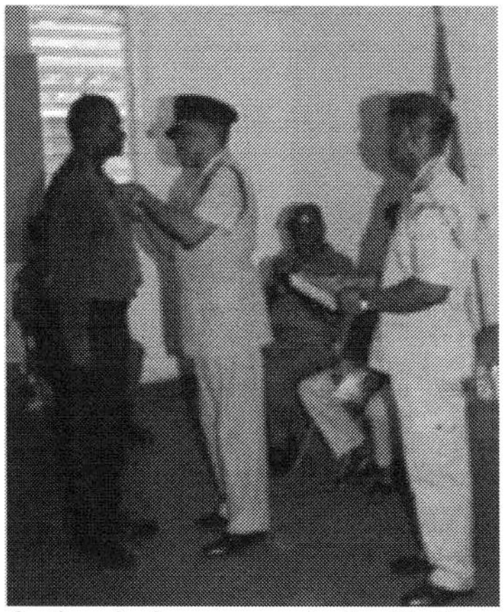

Author being presented with the Dominica Revival Medal.

I was able to visit the course and see the progress made. I attended the Closing Ceremony at which I was presented with the Dominica Cadet Revival Medal - a very special honour.

Major Richards and I participated in a radio interview, which sensitized the public to the progress made by the Dominica Cadet Corps and the role of the Barbados Cadet Corps at home.

This was my first visit to Dominica since 1974. My return had taken thirty-three years, and it was a nostalgic moment. I specifically asked to be taken to Camp Londonderry to show my wife where I spent time as a cadet.

Eartha and I at Camp Londonderry.

WO 2 Cherrol Deane tests the water.

With Captain Browne, Warrant Officer Deane, Sergeant Broomes and Captain Dorsen Robin of the Dominica Cadet Corps, Eartha and I visited the Fresh Water Lake where hot and cold streams of water were pouring out side by side. The vegetation was awe-inspiring and the air was crisp and pure. At an elevation of 3,000 feet above sea level, we were literally walking in the clouds.

Eartha pointing to the lovely flower

Eartha walking in the clouds

Major Francis, his wife Daphne, Eartha and I became inseparable friends from that visit onwards.

Course participants from the Dominica Cadet Corps posing for a photo with instructors from Cadet Headquarters. Seated (left to right): Captain Dennis Browne, Commandant, Lieutenant Colonel Trevor Browne, CEO, Major Patrick Skeete and Captain Maria Moore. Standing: BDF Cadet HQ staff. (Second from right) WO 2 Ferdie Smith. (Standing extreme right) Sgt. Gregory Broome.

In 2008, we provided training on the Potential Officers' Course for ten Dominicans. This was very significant, as countries tended to send only two officers to the course.

As previously mentioned, the relationship between the Barbados Cadet Corps and the Dominica Cadet Corps goes back to 1939 when my former English teacher of the 1960s took a group of cadets to Dominica. At that time, even the Headmaster, Rev. Armstrong, commented on the relationship, as I noted in my first book, "The Combermere Cadet," when he said "The boys enjoyed themselves thoroughly...The Dominicans spared no pains to make the boys happy."

I also experienced this level of hospitality extended by personnel of the Dominica Cadet Corps.

30

Assistance to Grenada

The first time I attended the Caribbean Commandants' Conference was in St. Lucia, in 1994. When I returned for the 2009 Conference, I met Mr. Charles George, who later became Commandant of the Grenada Cadet Corps. He was seeking assistance with the revival of the Grenada Cadet Corps, and from the moment he made the request, I started thinking of ways to help.

Major Charles George

To get their syllabus started, I supplied him with training materials, and conceptualized a mission to Grenada for our Star 4 cadets.

Having gained approval from the Defence Board, through the Defence Force, the mission commenced at 1915 hours on Wednesday, July 20, 2010. Star 4 cadets left the base at Paragon for HMBS PELICAN, where they boarded the vessel for the nine-hour journey to Grenada and the start of their adventurous training exercise. Staff members from Cadet Headquarters and parents waved goodbye from the dock, as HMBS RUDYARD LEWIS set sail at 2200 hours with cadets and their adult leaders standing proudly on deck in their uniforms and life vests. Leading the group was Major John Walcott, who was assisted by OCdt. Zara Massiah, officer in charge of the

Cadets on Board the HMBS Preparing to Depart for Grenada.

females; Sergeant Samuel Boyce, Permanent Staff Instructor at Cadet Headquarters; and BDF medic, Pte. Small S.

On the morning after the first group left by sea, the remainder of the contingent assembled at the Grantley Adams International Airport to travel to Grenada under the leadership of 2nd Lieutenant Khalil Greene and Officer Cadet Tikesia Clarke. After checking in, the cadets were assembled for prayers with Rev. Devere Murrell, BDF chaplain. Witnessing their departure along with parents and well-wishers were Commandant, Lt. Col. Trevor Browne and Deputy Chief of Staff, Lt. Col. Atheline Branch.

Two days before the groups left Barbados, an advance party comprising Captain Errol Brathwaite and a BDF cook, Pte. Daniel, flew to Grenada to prepare for their arrival.

The Star 4 Cadets were expected to serve as instructors and role models for the new cadets of the recently reconstituted Grenada Cadet Corps. This was a very special role to play in the revival of an organization that had been inactive since the 1980's.

Sgt. Samuel Boyce conducting a drill lesson with Grenadian cadets.

Both Major Walcott and Major Charles George later confirmed that, in keeping with the objective, leadership opportunities were provided for our Star 4 cadets to function effectively as NCOs. To this end, they served rotationally as Platoon Commanders, Section Commanders, Duty Sergeants and Corporals and acted as instructors and assessors. The Star 4s were well prepared from Barbados and the

Route march in Grenada.

quality of instruction and leadership they displayed was good and, in some cases, outstanding.

A series of television interviews was conducted by the local media. Sgt. Christine Fieldler represented Barbados in the first interview on Thursday, July 22, which focused on the senior NCOs from each country. The other interviews targeting the officers were recorded on the following day, and Major Walcott spoke on behalf of the Barbados contingent.

On the following Sunday morning, the cadets demonstrated their skills publicly in parades and route marches after two church services at St Patrick's Anglican in Seauters in the North and St David's Catholic at Corinth in the South. The displays delighted the residents in the two districts, many of whom came out of their houses to see the cadets when they heard the loud words of command which were piercing the air. The celebrating priest for St. Patrick's took the salute for the March Past.

Barbadian cadets supervising the Grenadian cadets on the adventurous training exercise.

Codenamed "Red Spice," the Adventurous Training Exercise took the cadets from Happy Hill School to Annandale, along a route which was, for the most part, off the main road. The trek consisted of eight miles of scenic tranquility, with an uphill climb that got progressively steeper. Major Walcott noted his pride in the cadets who completed the journey in half the time estimated.

Prime Minister Tillman Thomas taking the salute on the March Past

A closing ceremony and parade were held at the camp at 0900 hours on Wednesday 28, under Major George's command. The Prime Minister of Grenada, the Hon. Tillman Thomas, took the salute as the main dignitary in attendance, and presented certificates of participation to local and visiting senior adult ranks and officers. He was accompanied by other ministers of his cabinet, including the

Ministers of Education and Foreign Affairs. There were also other high ranking government officials in attendance including a senior officer of the Grenada Police Force.

According to reports, the Prime Minister also thanked the training teams from Trinidad and Tobago, Jamaica and Barbados for their effort and willingness to help re-establish the GCC following its thirty-year hiatus.

Major Walcott also noted the "broad smiles on the faces of our Star 4 cadets and adult ranks," who quietly acknowledged the kudos for their role in elevating the standards of Grenadian cadets.

Grenada revisited in 2011

We achieved great progress in helping to revive the Grenada Cadet Corps in 2010, but there was still more work to be done. The following year, Major Charles George made a second request for assistance. The Defence Board approved the request through the BDF.

A contingent of fifteen master cadets and six adult officers from the Barbados Cadet Corps travelled to Grenada from July 20-27, 2011, and set up camp at Happy Hill Secondary School, St. George's.

From their base of operation, the Barbadians set about their task, assisting the Grenada Cadet Corps (GCC) with training for cadets and adults. This involved assisting with the training of GCC Star 2 cadets, and testing them in drill, skill at arms, field craft and map and compass. The Barbadian instructors were also required to conduct training for the GCC's Potential and Under Officers.

Five officers from the Barbados Cadet Corps participated in this camp: namely, Capt. Errol Brathwaite; Lt. Wayne Hinds; Lieutenant Lincoln Springer; 2Lt. Donovan Smith; 2Lt Mary Walker; Sgt. Samuel Boyce, and a BDF medic. The BDF also supplied an experienced cook - Private Daniel.

Captain Brathwaite later confirmed that the training objectives were met during the camp. He noted that the Grenadian Star 2 cadets were trained and tested in drill, skill at arms, map and compass and field craft by Lt. Lincoln Springer and his team. Training for Potential Officers included modules on Leadership, Methods of Instruction, Defence Writing, Public Speaking and Unit Administration.

Captain Brathwaite also reported that there were two church services on Sunday, July 17, which were attended by all members of the contingent. Route marches were performed through both districts, where the respective priests took the salutes.

A Closing Ceremony was held on the morning of Wednesday, July 27, at 0900 hours. Several government officials were in attendance, chief among whom was the Prime Minister of Grenada, the Hon. Tillman Thomas, who took the salute.

Certificates of participation were presented to all the attendees at camp. Major Charles George later informed me that he was extremely pleased with the assistance and support he received throughout the exercise.

Travel on LIAT to Grenada from Barbados was uneventful, but the return trip was challenging because industrial action by the pilots caused several interruptions to the regular flight schedule.

Our officers were trained to recognize when it was necessary to involve Cadet Headquarters. Contingent Commanders and their support staff were capable of dealing with issues, generally. However, this type of situation concerning the well-being of the cadets required direction from Cadet Headquarters and the involvement of the BDF.

When I received an overseas call from Capt. Brathwaite, I immediately thought of the parents and how they would react if their children seemed to be in danger of being stranded overseas. Moreover, funds were likely to be exhausted within a few days, and the Grenada Cadet Corps could not be expected to bear the expense in a protracted situation. Capt. Brathwaite indicated that they could possibly have secured a flight to Trinidad, but there were no flights to Barbados directly from Grenada. The BDF made arrangements for them to stay in a hotel near the airport in Trinidad and they paid for accommodation using the Contingency Fund. It was fortunate that we had increased that fund that year. The contingency fund was to be spent in emergencies and special, dire circumstances such as this one.

There was no greater feeling of relief than to see the cadets safely back at home after such turmoil.

Much emphasis has been placed on explaining the planning and execution of the Grenada mission to show how meticulous one has to be when dealing with children travelling overseas. I explained this in an effort to chronicle the planning and organization involved in arranging overseas camps like this one. It may have appeared to be an easy task, but it required a great deal of effort by many people.

Children's lives were involved and parents expected that they would be cared for and returned home safely. That was uppermost in our minds when we planned and executed activities.

Every year, between July and August, approximately 500 to 700 cadets would take part in various phases of camp. These included hiking through rough terrain, swimming, climbing hills, riding bicycles and travelling by boat or airplane. Whenever my cell phone rang, I always prayed that it would not be bad news. At the end of the camp phases, I always felt as though a burden had been lifted off my shoulders; it was a relief to return the children safely into the arms of their parents or guardians.

31

Assistance to St Vincent and the Grenadines Cadet Force

Lt. Col. Dwight Lewis.

Capt. Maria Moore, Capt. Delisle Bascombe and the author.

CSgt. David Knight (front row left) sitting among SVGCF personnel.

Lt. Col. Dwight Lewis, Commandant of the St. Vincent and the Grenadines Cadet Force (SVGCF) requested assistance with training. After approval by the Defence Board, a training plan was prepared by the Barbados Cadet Corps in collaboration with the SVGCF.

I headed the team from Cadet Headquarters which conducted a Train-The-Trainers' programme for their officers and NCOs. Also on the team

WO2 Ferdie Smith (BDF) teaching sword drill to officers of the SVGCF.

Receiving the Caribbean Cadet Medal from the Governor-General of St. Vincent and the Grenadines.

were Capt. Delisle Bascombe, Capt. Maria Moore, WO 2 Ferdie Smith, Colour Sgt. David Knight and Sgt. Christopher Walker. The Barbados Cadet Association Inc. funded the exercise.

It was easy to work with Lieutenant Colonel Lewis. In 1991, when I rejoined the Barbados Cadet Corps, I read a document that he had written, and agreed wholeheartedly with his training philosophy. I therefore knew his intent and assisted in the process.

Training targeted three categories of personnel in the SVGCF: namely, the officers, the Potential Officers and twenty senior cadets. St Vincent and the Grenadines were hosting the Caribbean Cadet Camp in July 2008, and this training was ideal for boosting their capabilities.

In providing training for our Caribbean neighbours, we were developing their skills, while building our own capacity and exposing Barbadian Cadets to different environments.

It was a pleasure working alongside Capt. Vulon Layne and Capt. Idelia Ferdinand, who were both trained in Barbados on Potential Officers' courses, with which I was associated.

These were all duties far beyond the desk. Technically, they were not part of the script when I undertook the job at Cadet Headquarters.

On the recommendation of Commandants throughout the region, I received the Caribbean Cadet Medal for assistance rendered to Caribbean countries. The Governor-General of St. Vincent presented the medal as part of the activities for the Caribbean Cadet Commandants' Conference 2008. The driving force behind it all was Lt. Col. Dwight Lewis.

32

Caribbean Cadet Commandants' Conference

1994: Participants in the Training Officers Conference. Front row (L-R): Author, Major Trevor McCurdy and Major Edison Isaac.

In 1994, I accompanied Lt. Col. R Clarke to the Caribbean Commandants' Conference in St. Lucia, and attended the Closing Parade in Dennery.

This may have been the first time that there was a training conference held as part of the event. The idea was to have the Training Officers meet and review training and then the Commandants would set the policy, based on their input. It was at that conference that I first met the then Major Trevor McCurdy (Jamaica Combined Cadet Force) and Major Edison Isaac (Trinidad and Tobago Cadet Force). This meeting, chaired by Lt. Cyril Saltibus of the St. Lucia Cadet Corps, was a significant development in regional "cadetting."

In 1995, I accompanied Lt. Col. Clarke to the conference in Trinidad and Tobago, where I met Colonel George Sebro from Trinidad and Colonel Ben Francis from Jamaica. These men were excellent leaders and role models, and it was a pleasure to join them at breakfast and interact with them as they took part in the conference. I was steadily being initiated into my new role of Staff Officer.

I accompanied Lt. Col. Owen Springer to St. Vincent in 1996, when I met another strong leader, the now Colonel Lindo, Commandant of Jamaica Combined Cadet Corps.

Barbados hosted the Caribbean Cadet Camp and the Commandants' Conference in 1997. Commandants from Antigua, Anguilla, St Kitts and Nevis, St. Vincent, St. Lucia, St. Vincent and the Grenadines, Trinidad and Tobago, Jamaica, and Belize met in the Central Liason Office of Paragon for the Conference. Participating in the camp that year was a British Army Cadet Force unit led by Major Mark Andrews. Major Andrews, who had previously lived in Barbados, was allowed to attend the Opening

Commandants and Senior Officers from Antigua, United Kingdom, Anguilla, Canada, St Kitts and Nevis, St Vincent, St. Lucia, St. Vincent and the Grenadines, Trinidad and Tobago, Jamaica, Belize and Host country Barbados.

Ceremony as an observer. Also in attendance was Major Alex Moseanu from Canada, who routinely attended the conferences. As Commandant of the Barbados Cadet Corps, Lt. Col. Springer presided. It was one of the biggest Commandants' Conferences ever.

For the 2004 conference, which fell during our centenary celebrations, I felt that we needed to make the public aware of what was taking place. I noted previously that in other countries, the conference would be held in a room and, quite often, the public was not aware of it. I therefore organized a special Opening Ceremony with media coverage at Hotel Pommarine, where the delegates were staying. Present were the Minister of Education, the Hon Reginald Farley; the Chief Education Officer, Mrs. Wendy Griffith-Watson; former Chief of Staff, Col. Leonard Banfield; Lt. Col. Florence Gittens; and a number of former Commandants. The Principal of a secondary school in Grenada also attended as an observer.

The conference opened with cadets carrying the flags of their respective countries into the room. Following were speeches by the Commandant, Lt. Col. T. Browne; the Chief of Staff, Col. Alvin Quintyne; and the Minister of Education. I was Master of Ceremonies for the event, which was very well received and marked the beginning of this type of approach to the conferences.

Barbadian and Jamaican cadets beating drums at the opening ceremony.

I also felt that we needed to have a formal annual handover of duties among Commandants. Traditionally, the Commandant of the country hosting the Caribbean Cadet Camp would serve as Chairman of the Commandants' Conference. With this in mind, I purchased a crystal orb to be used prior to the start of the conferences to symbolize the transfer of responsibilities. The orb was introduced at the 2004 conference in Barbados with the intention that it would be taken to the various countries for the conference and help to generate publicity around the event.

Handing over the orb to Col. Edison Isaac

In 2005, I was seated on a plane to Trinidad with the orb, which was to be presented to Col. Edison Isaac at the airport. When we reached PIARCO International, we were received in the VIP Lounge where many senior officers from the participating countries were waiting to witness the brief ceremony. There was a round of applause when I handed over the orb, and I thought then that we were moving in the right direction by formalizing this process.

Commandants, Training Officers and other senior officers from Regional Cadet Forces gather in the VIP Lounge at PIARCO International Airport to witness the formal handover of the ORB.

I believed that this approach would generate the publicity necessary to make the public aware that something important was taking place and draw greater attention to the Cadet Corps.

Lieutenant Colonel Trevor Browne and I attended that 2005 Conference.

2006 was a very busy year for me. It was the year I journeyed to Canada to see the facilities and personnel where our officers were being trained. When I returned, I was busy with administration for local and overseas camps to be held simultaneously in different countries. I was therefore unable to attend the Commandants' Conference in Jamaica. Major Irvin Boyce attended instead.

Lt. Col. T Browne and author – Commandants' Conference 2005

I represented the Commandant at the Commandants' Conferences in St. Vincent in 2008, St. Lucia in 2009, Trinidad in 2010 and Grand Cayman in 2012. Major Peter Powlett accompanied me to St. Vincent in 2008, and in 2009, I was accompanied by Capt. Dennis Browne, Training Coordinator at Cadet Headquarters. I was unaccompanied in 2010 when the conference was held at the Hyatt Hotel in Port of Spain, but in 2012, Major Errol Brathwaite attended with me in Grand Cayman.

The main objective was to expose as many of our senior officers of the conference as possible.

The Barbados Cadet Corps undertook to stage the 2011 conference in Barbados, when it was clear that the country which was originally slated to host could no longer do so. Thanks to the hard work put in by Capt. Dennis Browne and his staff, the conference was organized at very short notice. It was held in Hodgson Hall of the Barbados Defence Force. Afterwards, the Commandants and other participants had lunch in the Barbados Defence Force Officers' Mess, before attending the Cosing Ceremony for the International Cadet Challenge Camp.

Earlier in the visit, the Commandants witnessed the Drill Competition, which was held outside the Garfield Sobers Gymnasium.

Leading up to the conference, I had the pleasure of a visit to Barbados by Colonel Patrick Taylor, the new Commandant of the Trinidad and Tobago Cadet Force.

Words cannot express the true value of these conferences in terms of my own personal exposure and development. At every conference, we represented the interests of both the Barbados Cadet Corps and the region. The conferences provided fantastic networking opportunities.

The conference in the Cayman Islands was special to me, as it was my last. It was also a chance to see first-hand what progress had been made in Grand Cayman in terms of the Cadet Corps' development and to say farewell to my Caribbean colleagues. The Commandants included Colonel Lemuel Lindo (Jamaica Combined Cadet Force); Colonel Patrick Taylor (Trinidad and Tobago Cadet Force); Lieutenant Colonel Dwight Lewis (St. Vincent and the Grenadines Cadet Force); Lieutenant Colonel Glyne Dunnah (Antigua and Barbuda National Cadet Corps); Lieutenant Colonel

Charles George (Grenada Cadet Corps); Lieutenant Colonel Bobeth O'Garro (Cayman Islands Cadet Corps); and Captain Dorsen Robin, (Dominica Cadet Corps). Captain Grantley Dick was at the conference and so too was Capt. Wallace Williams of the Trinidad and Tobago Cadet Force.

It was ironic that Captain Dick and I were at the same conference. As young cadets, we both attended the Canadian Exchange Caribbean camp in Barbados in 1973. He recalled the names of cadets who were at that camp, and we reaffirmed our bond which surpassed our jobs as Cadet Executive Officers. We were passionate about preserving the history of the Corps/Force and shared an interest in protocol. I have always enjoyed these discussions with him.

I also relished the idea of meeting with Commandants and Training Officers to talk about the progress made in standardizing training and ensuring that the Caribbean Camp and Commandants' Conference were preserved.
As tributes were being offered, country by country, Commandant by Commandant, I felt a great sense of accomplishment knowing that my life's work had meant something to others outside of Barbados. For assisting the Cayman Islands, I received their 10th Anniversary Award in Grand Cayman in 2012. I thanked Lt. Col. O'Garro and her personnel for the very kind gesture.

33

Lack of Medals and Decorations

To date, no medals were issued to Cadet Corps officers. At no time was this more evident than at the Commandants' Conference in Grand Cayman when a young Lieutenant from one of the Caribbean cadet forces said quietly, "I have heard about you for a long time. I notice that you have no medals on your uniform besides your Caribbean Cadet Medal. Don't they issue medals in your country?" Of course, all the other officers were wearing their medals proudly.

However, this does not mean that our officers are less worthy of honour than others throughout the "cadetting" world, who are awarded for their contribution and years of service. Admittedly, I was uncomfortable when the question was asked, but it is not too late for the local authorities to redress the situation for existing and future officers.

Nevertheless, we were determined that until the system recognized the contribution of Cadet Corps officers, we would find ways to honour our own.

We therefore submitted names for Defence Board Commendations in 2005 and 2006, but knew that these could never truly replace the award of medals. At least eight officers, including myself, were awarded Defence Board Commendations.

We also held celebratory dinners for officers who had contributed twenty-one years or more of dedicated service. These functions were held at the Hilton Barbados and the honourees were presented with red velvet cases, each containing a special cane with the officer's name inscribed on it.

In 2005, we invited Major Andre Mathurin, Commandant of St. Lucia Cadet Corps, to join us. I was one of the honourees, along with Lieutenant Colonel Browne, Lieutenant Commander Carl Farley, Major James Bradshaw and Major Irvin Boyce.

(L-R) Major John Morodore, Capt. Randolph Charles, Capt. George Vaughn, Major Peter Powlett and Major Dwight Lewis.

In the following year, June 2006, the honourees were Major Peter Powlett and Captains John Morodore, David Clarke, George Vaughan and Randolph Charles. The Corps also invited Major Dwight Lewis, Commandant of the St. Vincent and the Grenadines Cadet Force to receive an award for twenty-one years of service to the SVGCF. Both Major Mathurin and Major Lewis had completed the Potential Officers' Course in Barbados in 1984 and 1985 respectively.

The Minister of Education was the main dignitary on both occasions.

We also presented plaques to officers who had given twelve years of dedicated service. Interestingly, other officers in the system received medals after the same period of time. The dinners and awards were all funded by Cadet Corps officers.

Lt. Col T Browne welcome guests at the Appreciation Ceremony

Guests Lt. Col Neville Edwards and Lt (CG) Vince Dottin

Left to right: Commandant, Lt Col Trevor Browne, Cdr. Wilbert Kirton, Lt. Col. Clyde Parris, Lt. Col Owen Springer and Lt. Col. Jeffrey Bostic.

In 2007, the Commandant, Lt. Col T. Browne, went one stage further by asking me to organize a ceremony in the form of a cocktail reception at the BDF Officers' Mess. It was aimed not only at recognizing the efforts of officers who had given 12 years or more of service, but, additionally, benefactors of the Corps were invited to join the officers for a special treat to thank them for their contributions during the year.

There was an overwhelming response to this initiative. The large number of persons who attended made it a very worthwhile exercise. Among the guests were Deputy Chief of Staff, Cdr. Wilbert Kirton, former Commandants Lt Col. Neville Edwards and Lt. Col. Owen Springer. Lt Col. Jeffrey Bostic and Lt. Col. Clyde Parris were also there in their capacity as former Staff Officer Cadets. They, too, had done their tour of duty in Cadet Headquarters and had paved the way for me – a fact for which I will be eternally grateful.

The Cadet Band provided the background music on a truly splendid evening of entertainment. Their parents and those of the sea cadets were also invited to participate.

My 50th Birthday Celebration

The momentum created by the intense focus on ensuring that children are kept busy with activities can tend to make one think less about any personal considerations. However, it is energizing to have others show some measure of appreciation for your efforts from time to time. It fuels your desire to reach even further forward and give more of yourself. Those of us who are involved in youth work and, indeed, in activities which require a great deal of voluntary effort, know very well that we do it for the sake of our children's development. We know that the satisfaction will come later when we see them mature into worthwhile citizens, not only of Barbados, but of the world. While we are taking care of others, it is also important that someone, somewhere, remembers to also take care of us. This being said, I therefore am grateful to the Commandant, Lt. Col. Trevor Browne, and Officers of the Corps who in 2006, decided to honour me by staging a 50th Birthday function for me.

Author with wife, Eartha, and daughters Janelle and Gemma

It was a wonderful fiftieth birthday celebration. It was held at the Main Guard.

My wife Eartha and I were brought by chauffeur to the venue, where we were greeted by the Commandant and by Officers and their guests. Lt. Michael Boyce was the Liaison Officer who accompanied us in the vehicle. The chauffeur was Sgt. Wendell Kellman, a Permanent Staff Instructor at Cadet Headquarters.

My children were present and so too were my siblings, Steve and Patricia, and their children.

I felt honoured that they would provide such a festivity on my behalf. I am very thankful to Lt. Col. Browne and my fellow officers for this very kind gesture.

Author and wife with Major Margot Greene, Mrs. Sandie Kellman, and Ms. Jessica Ashby (former student at Combermere School)

Author with Major Peter Powlett

Author's daughter Janelle with cousins Kris Carrington, Kay Carrington and Gregory Skeete

34

State Partnership Youth Programme Exchange

In September 2007, Major Sean Reece, who was G1 in BDF Headquarters at the time, called to tell me about an offer to visit St. Croix and Florida to see a number of youth programmes. I was one of two people from Barbados selected to go. The other person was a Sergeant Roland Cobbler of the Royal Barbados Police Force.

The State Partnership Youth Programme Subject Matter Expert Exchange was the second in a series of events focusing specifically on the youth. This initiative allowed for discussion on the youth and community service programmes run by the National Guard units of Florida and the US Virgin Islands. Representatives from the defense and police forces, and youth programme directors from Barbados and Antigua and Barbuda participated in the exchange.

Seated at Grantley Adams International Airport with Sgt. Roland Cobbler (leaning over)

We left Barbados for Puerto Rico, and then took a connecting flight to St. Croix, US Virgin Islands. Colonel Adams, of the US Virgin Islands (USVI) National Guard, met us at the airport. Based on the discussion in the vehicle as we drove from the airport, I realized that St. Croix was experiencing the same problems with young people as other countries. It was interesting to see how their approach compared with ours. We attended a seminar in the city (Christiansted) and presentations were made by the leaders of various youth movements associated with the USVI National Guard and Police Force.

After each session, participants were given an opportunity to ask questions. Having the Barbados Cadet Corps International Cadet Challenge Camp (ICCC) video made it easy to do a presentation, which was both concise and visually appealing. The reaction was overwhelming, and the delegates wanted to see it a second time. The video not only highlighted what the BCC was doing in terms of training, it also showcased cadets from around the region. This gave the USVI personnel an idea of what young people of similar ethnic and historical backgrounds were achieving.

Orientation in Florida

On Wednesday, September 12, 2007, our group comprising representatives from Antigua and Barbuda, Barbados and the US Virgin Islands left St. Croix for Puerto Rico to take a connecting flight to Miami International Airport. From Miami, we took another flight to Jacksonville Florida, where we were met by an officer of the Florida National Guard (FLNG). The final stop was a hotel in St Augustine.

On Friday, September 14, we saw the work being done at the Florida Youth Challenge Academy (FLYCA), which proved to be the most interesting of the programmes we observed throughout the tour.

FLYCA students rock climbing.

Eartha with Jenny and Wendell

Author with brother-in-law Wendell

The FLYCA targets students between the ages of sixteen to eighteen; so called "at risk students," who have not yet committed felonies, but who are dropouts and are coping with numerous challenges, including drug abuse and delinquent behavior. The FYLCA accommodates 250 students twice each year. The programme engages the youth in a two-week orientation stint, similar to boot camp, followed by eighteen weeks of residential training. After that, there is a one-year period of job attachments and follow-up activities. These cadets wear military uniform like the Barbados Youth Service, and are required to do their own laundry. Besides the military training, they do vocational subjects and complete their High School Education.

The orientation was an excellent opportunity to network with people who were all working at finding solutions for developing strength of character in young people.

I had to pass through Miami International Airport en route from Jacksonville. I had applied for vacation leave to spend time with my sister and her husband Wendell who live in Loxahatchee, Florida.

My wife Eartha joined me there and we had a wonderful time with Jenny and Wendell at their home. It is always pleasing to be in the company of my sister Jenny. I also enjoyed playing scrabble with Wendell who plays in tournaments. I never won any of these games, but it whetted my appetite for scrabble which I now play on line against opponents from different countries.

It was a welcome break from what was, for me, a very hectic daily routine as CEO of the Cadet Corps.

35

Partnership with the Directorate of Cadets Canada

From as far back as the days of the Caribbean Canadian Exchange Camps, the Barbados Cadet Corps always enjoyed a good rapport with the officials of the Canadian cadet system. Lt. Col. Deighton Maynard played a significant role in finding opportunities for training and orientation prior to 2006.

In the mid-1990s, Major Margot Greene and Potential Cadet Officer Philip Eno were sent to Canada to visit the training bases. There they met Capt. Bruce Covington, who was very helpful and provided them with a great deal of training materials.

When Lt. Col. Browne became Commandant, he was concerned about officers' training and the absence of courses in Barbados. Since 1984, there were no consistent qualification courses for officers other than the Potential Officers' and Range Authorization courses. Occasionally, there were First Aid courses and sessions in various elements of training. There were no qualifying courses above the level of Potential Officer.

Therefore, in 2006, Lt. Col. Browne contacted the cadet authorities in Canada, where he had done his Basic Officer Qualification in 1973 at CFB London Ontario and attended summer camp at Gagetown in 1971.

After an informative telephone discussion with the head of the Regional Cadet Instructor School, we were offered an opportunity to take part in courses at some of the Canadian Cadet Training Centres. The courses were intended to upgrade the skills of our officers and standardize their procedures. In my opinion, this was a giant leap in our development. I was overjoyed!

Six Officers were selected for training that year: Potential Cadet Officer Debra Dreana Marshall (Basic Officer Course); Potential Cadet Officer Khalil Greene and Second Lieutenant Junior Ward (Lieutenant Qualification Course); Lieutenants Michael Boyce and Lincoln Springer (Captain Qualification Course); and Sub Lieutenant Robert Morris (Military Occupational Course [Sea] for Navy Cadet Instructor Cadre Officers).

Lt. Col. Browne felt that it was important for me to visit Canada and build a relationship with the Canadian cadet personnel and observe the officers on course. My visit was approved by the Barbados Defence Force Headquarters for June 2006.

Major Irvin Boyce of the Barbados Cadet Corps taking Parish Ambassadors on an early morning hike.

I was honoured to stay at the residence of the Barbados High Commissioner in Ottawa. His Excellency Glyne Murray, who was High Commissioner at the time, showered me with good Bajan hospitality. Senator Murray and I had developed a bond in 2000, when he attended a Cadet Corps promotional display on a pasture in Speightstown and was impressed with the survival training done by the young cadets. He called me a few days afterwards to say that he felt that type of training would be ideal for the Parish Ambassadors. The Parish Ambassadors are young men and women, who are chosen to represent each of the eleven parishes in Barbados. Working as couples, they

Author with HE Glyne Murray

compete every year in activities which showcase the positive aspects of youth in the community. Senator Murray asked me to create a schedule for a weekend of training. I was happy to comply. That training programme became a special feature of the Parish Ambassadors' experience for almost a decade. Many of the Parish Ambassadors have openly admitted that the survival training had helped them in their own professional development.

I even served as Chief Judge for the Parish Projects for a number of years. This activity drew us closer, thereby heightening the bond which had formed naturally as "brothers" in the Combermere fraternity.

On the first night spent at his residence, Eartha and I had just settled into our room, when His Excellency knocked at the door. There were chairs available, but he opted to sit on the floor and chat with us while we were sitting up in bed. We were amazed at his humility. His actions reminded me that, no matter what status one achieves in life, it is important not to lose the "common touch."

As previously arranged, Lieutenant Commander Peter McIntyre, head of the Regional Cadet Instructor School, collected me from the High Commissioner's residence. We travelled across Ontario, from Ottawa to Toronto, over a five-day period, stopping at military bases where cadet training centres were located. These included Connaught Ranges Summer Training Centre; HMCS Ontario in Kingston; Trenton Air Cadet Summer Training Centre; Borden, the Regional Cadet Support Unit Headquarters; and Blackdown Army Cadet Summer Training Centre.

Author With 2Lt Junior Ward and PCO Khalil Greene

At each location, I met with the officer in charge to explain our training philosophy and see the facilities where our officers would be trained.

I was fortunate to see some of the Barbadian Officers in their training setting. I took a photo with 2Lt Junior Ward and PCO Khalil Greene and then moved on to Trenton Air Cadet Training Centre.

L-R: LCdr. Peter McIntyre, Lieutenant. Lincoln Springer, Major Patrick Skeete, Lieutenant. Michael Boyce in the classroom at Trenton Base.

Eartha join us

At Trenton, where the Captain Qualification Course was taking place, I got a chance to see Lieutenants Boyce and Springer and observe a class in progress. I was very pleased with the standard of training. The Directorate of Cadets, Canada had sent us the training documents on a CD, and we had shared the information with the students, who were required to study the material before attending the course. We also gave our students a video of the Barbados Cadet Corps to share with their counterparts in Canada.

Throughout this entire exercise there were many aspects which gave me food for thought. The benefit of travelling to other countries and seeing how training is done is that it broadens one's horizons.

Author with Candice and Peter in Canada

Peter, his wife Candice, my wife Eartha and I developed a special friendship. They accommodated us at their home in Wasaga Beach. It was a great opportunity to build a strong friendship.

Peter Eartha, Candice, and me at a restaurant in Barbados

Less than a year later, we were fortunate to reciprocate when they stopped over in Barbados on a cruise. We collected them from the Bridgetown Port and took them to various places of interest. We made a special arrangement for them to tour the Coast Guard base and this was followed by a brief island tour.

Later in the afternoon, we went to a local restaurant for lunch. Commandant, Lt Col Browne, and a number of Officers who had received training in Canada joined us for lunch.

Everyone was eager to show Peter how much they appreciated efforts made by him and his team back in Canada. Eventually, it was time to rejoin the ship to continue the cruise and we bid a fond farewell to Peter and Candice.

Peter and Candice continue to be special friends whom we contact from time to time.

2006: LCdr Peter McIntryre and his wife Candice pose with (L-R) PCO Dreana Marshall, 2Lt Junior Ward,PCO Khalil Greene, Lt Col Trevor Browne, Lt Lincoln Springer and Lt. Michael Boyce.

Standing (centre) with Major Alex Moseanu and Major Russ Mayne (in the foreground).

We also spent two days at Major Russ Mayne's home in Mississauga. He took us to an indoor parade function at his unit, at which Major Alex Moseanu, who had visited Barbados many times and was a friend of our Cadet Corps, was present. Major Mayne visited Barbados in 1997 for our local camp and in 1999, he hosted nineteen of our cadets at his home, turning his backyard into a campsite. A good and reliable friend, he returned in 2004 for our centennial camp and visited my home.

Lt. Col Tom McNeil (extreme right) chats with (L-R) Capt. Maria Moore, Capt. Randolph Clarke and Lt. Col. T.T. Browne.

Our friendship was such that on one occasion, he asked my daughter Alicia, who was studying at the University of Toronto, to visit his unit and present an award to one of his cadets. Also, whenever she was returning to Barbados for summer vacation, Russ allowed her to leave her belongings at his home.

In 2009, we invited a team of Canadian officers to come to Barbados to deliver training modules. This meant that more officers could be trained at a lower cost. We contacted Lieutenant Colonel McNeil and Lieutenant Commander Peter Kay, the former of whom subsequently did a reconnaissance to Barbados to set up the course. Later, a team of officers, including Lieutenant Commander Kay and Captains Brice Castle and Kony Trudel came to Barbados to conduct the course at the Coast Guard Base, HMBS PELICAN.

The local officers who participated in this Advanced Leadership Course found it to be interesting and useful.

It is note-worthy therefore that between 2006 and 2009, more than twenty officers were trained in Canada and training was provided for twenty-two in Barbados.

This relationship with the Canadian Cadet system was for me, another exciting administrative activity. By now, I was thoroughly enjoying the new arenas in which we were engaged.

36

100th Anniversary of the Canadian Cadet Instructor Cadre

Another high point in my career occurred in 2009. The Directorate of Cadets, Canada was celebrating the 100th Anniversary of the Cadet Instructor Cadre and was holding a professional development seminar. We were given invitations for four of our officers to join approximately 160 others from across Ontario. The seminar started in Rigaud, Quebec, on December 10, 2009. The prospect of being in Quebec in December in the freezing cold was not at all inviting, but the thought of participating in the conference was exciting, and we were prepared for the challenge. Major Peter Powlett, Major David Clarke and Captain Delisle Bascombe were the other three members of the team.

When we stepped outside the airport terminal, it was very cold and snow was falling. I had never seen snow before and it was like entering a massive freezer.

Barbadian officers in warm clothing.

Brunch at the High Commissioner's Residence.

Friend from French Canada presenting me with a flag.

Luckily, we were prepared with warm clothing. Lieutenant (Naval) Paul Fraser from the Directorate of Cadets, Canada picked us up and took us first to the residence of the then Barbados High Commissioner, His Excellency Evelyn Greaves, before going on to Rigaud. We received a warm welcome at the High Commissioner's residence, and were treated to an Independence Day Brunch. Present were the Barbados Tourism Representative in Ottawa, and the President of the Barbados Ottawa Association, Ms. Sandra Asgill, who is herself a former cadet. Another former cadet and student of mine, Ms. Christabelle Reece, who worked at the High Commission, was also there as was Mr. Derek Clarke, a former band member of No. 3 Company.

We really enjoyed the Bajan hospitality in Ottawa and thought that it was truly a good start to our trip.

The seminar focused on professional development and methods of motivating and training cadets, using various methods.

On the first night of the conference, I was given an opportunity to address the gathering about the Barbados Cadet Corps. My presentation contained video clips of our west and east coastlines, the Parliament buildings, Bridgetown and the Warrens industrial complex. They also showed glimpses of our Cadet Corps; its history and role in developing society, and the part the Canadians played in the process over the years. Noting that there were French Canadians in the group, I gave my opening greetings in both French and English.

Chatting with senior cadets of the Governor General's Horse Guards Cadet Unit.

Cadets preparing shelters at Connaught Ranges.

The next day, one of the members of the French group presented me with a flag and a cap in appreciation of my effort to reach out to them.

It was pleasing to see the flags of Barbados and the Barbados Cadet Corps on the platform with the Canadian flag.

Lieutenant Colonel Tom McNeil and his wife Jennifer arranged a special visit to her unit, where I met the cadets affiliated with the Governor-General's Foot Guards. I inspected the cadets and spoke to them about acquiring both military and life skills and, as requested, stressed the importance of good deportment. Afterwards, I showed the videos which I had shown at the conference, to the senior cadets, the adult leaders, parents and sponsors.

It was always exciting to speak with cadets from other countries and recognize that they had the same passion as those in Barbados. The group wanted to come to Barbados in March of the following year on an exchange with our Corps, and we held preliminary discussions. I was delighted to have the opportunity to explain to parents and cadets how our system worked. Later, it was clear that my visit reassured them, because the exchange became a reality.

BCC officers paying courtesy call on Director, Col. Craig Fletcher

We also had an opportunity to see the cadets in the field and observe as they set up shelters and prepared meals.

In addition, we were taken to the Headquarters of the Directorate of Cadets, Canada, to pay a courtesy call on the Director of Cadets,

Colonel Craig Fletcher, to whom we presented a miniature sword with an inscription which showed appreciation to the Directorate of Cadets Canada for their hospitality. We were permitted to address the staff and I briefed them on the programme in Barbados and thanked them for the support they had given so far.

At the Closing Ceremony, we were also invited to go on stage for a final farewell. We thanked everyone and, as we left the stage, we showed a video of Barbados from the Tourism Authority. It was very well received, and we extended an open invitation to everyone to come to Barbados. In that regard, we were ambassadors for our country performing duties beyond the desk.

LCdr. Peter McIntyre joins us for a photo

It was pleasing to see my friend LCdr. Peter McIntyre at this conference.

One aspect of the Canadian cadet system which we in Barbados could examine more closely is how they make use of their retired officers. They use creative ways to incorporate them into the system, where they continue to influence the development of the youth organization.

Historic photo, December 5, 2009: BCC officers among others who paved the way: Left to Right - Major Peter Powlett, Major David Clarke, Capt. Kony Trudel, Lt. Cdr. Peter McIntyre, Lt. Col. Tom McNeil, Major Patrick Skeete, Capt. Brice Castle, Major Bruce Covington, Lt. Cdr. Peter Kay, Capt. Delisle Bascombe, Capt. Ken Gatehouse.

37

Reciprocal Visits Between Canadian and Barbadian Cadets

As a follow-up to my visit to Canada in 2009, the Governor-General's Foot Guards Cadets came to Barbados in 2010.

Major Buckler Freeman and Lieutenant Jennifer McNeil were the group leaders of the camp, which was held at our Paragon base from March 31 to April 6.

The visit was intended to foster a stronger bond between the Barbadians and Canadians and develop the framework for future cadet exchanges between the two units. The schedule featured a variety of challenging activities. These were interspersed with social and cultural activities to help the Canadians gain an appreciation for Barbadian culture.

On the first night of the camp, a welcome reception was held in association with the Canadian High Commission, which gave exemplary support to this activity.

Over the next week, Barbadian cadets who were camping with the Canadians were happy to offer their visiting counterparts the best of Bajan hospitality. The Canadian Cadets were treated to an island tour, with lunch at Bathsheba; a tour of the Barbados Coast Guard base at HMBS PELICAN; a visit to Harrison's Cave; and a ride on the local submarine.

We publicized the event through television and radio interviews on Mornin' Barbados and CBC Radio, respectively.

One of the highlights of the visit was a field training exercise, which took the Cadets down the very scenic walk from Cherry Tree Hill, passing Morgan Lewis Windmill, where the view is breathtaking even for Barbadians. They proceeded to Walkers and then to Barclays Park, where they set up shelters for the night.

Visit to Barbados by Director of Cadets Canada

The icing on the cake came when the Director of Cadets Canada, Col. Craig Fletcher, accepted an invitation to come to Barbados during that camp. He, too, was given a special welcome reception at my home with senior officers attending.

He visited the cadets while they were at Cherry Tree Hill on their adventurous training exercise, and he addressed them in the field.

He also visited the Barbados Cadet Corps Headquarters, where there were presentations by BDF personnel, Cadet Headquarters staff and Col. Fletcher himself, to familiarize everyone with their respective operating systems. However, the relationship between the BCC and Directorate of Cadets, Canada was the main focus.

Reciprocal visit by Barbadian Cadets to Canada.

Later that year, the 2784 Governor Generals Foot Guards Royal Canadian Army Cadet Corps (GGFG RCACC), the same unit that had come to Barbados in April, invited our master cadets to visit their camp in Canada, from August 21 to 28, 2010. The camp was held at the Connaught Camp site in Ottawa, and the Barbadians enjoyed themselves thoroughly. They learned from the experience and brought back memories, which they will cherish throughout their lives.

The selection of cadets for the exchange camp was based on specific criteria. The requirements were encompassed within their NCO training programme, which ran for a month prior to the start of the official NCO cadre camp. The NCOs were chosen on the strength of their performance and personal attitude. Eventually, fifteen cadets (twelve males and three females) were selected, ranging from CUO to the rank of Corporal.

We met several times with the contingent and their parents for about three weeks prior to their departure in order to mentally prepare them for their role as ambassadors for Barbados and to keep the parents up-to-date on information pertaining to their children's visit to Canada.

Three adult officers attended the exchange camp, and all of them played a critical and effective role in the success of the exchange. Capt. S. Norville ensured that the female cadets were well taken care of, while 2Lt. D. Gamble facilitated smooth communication between cadets and officers. Maj. R.M. Charles was the Contingent Commander.

Our objectives for this camp were to build stronger ties with the Canadians, and develop "espirit de corps." The camp allowed the Barbadian cadets to function confidently and effectively in another jurisdiction, and gave our CUOs and NCOs the opportunity to use their skills and training.

Brief Overview of Visit

The Barbados contingent was met on arrival by Lt. J. McNeal, OCdt A. Asboth, and some of the Canadian cadets who attended the Easter exchange camp in Barbados earlier in April. They were then transported to the Connaught base training facility via a school bus and escorted to their tents. The hospitality meted out to our Barbadian cadets was phenomenal. The Contingent Commander wrote in his After Action Report:

> On day one of our visit the cadets all woke up for 0600hrs as was common throughout the exchange, filed up and proceeded to the mess, which was a large, very spacious modern looking building approximately 300yds from our sleeping quarters. There we received our breakfast, lunch and dinner. Just to give you a short peek into our menu; there was a choice of about ten (10) different beverages (hot and cold), for breakfast there were eggs fried or scrambled, bacon, sausage, hash browns, warmed baked beans, pancakes with syrup, toast, cupcakes, choice of fruits and vegetables, for lunch there was rice (veg. or plain), cream potato, lasagna (beef or vegetable), chicken, fish, pork, vegetables and choice of fruit and for dinner we would have

baked potatoes, pasta, rice, chicken or pork, vegetables and a variety of pastry. We visited the very impressive war museum and went to a shopping mall in down town Ottawa. Afterwards we returned to base to prepare for themeet and greet which was hosted by Col. Fletcher.

Canadian and Barbadian cadets on their field training exercise.

Training included a field exercise and a brief lecture on wildlife; lighting and extinguishing the Coleman stove and lantern; erecting a shelter; and survival basics – ground to air signals. Most of the training was conducted by the Canadian NCO's.

38

Visit to the United Kingdom

We had established a good rapport with the Directorate of Cadets, Canada, and hosted a contingent of cadets from Nottinghamshire Army Cadet Force (ACF) at our International Cadet Challenge Camp. Lieutenant Colonel Browne thought I should go to the United Kingdom to build similar relations with their Army Cadet Forces.

Colonel Mike Reynolds.

We had already begun to build friendships with Nottinghamshire ACF. Col. Mike Reynolds, former Commandant of Nottinghamshire ACF was a regular visitor to Barbados, and it was through contact with him that the exchange between the Barbados Cadet Corps and Nottinghamshire Army Cadet Force was cemented.

It all began with his visit to me at this office, seeking an arrangement for an exchange. It was because of this visit that a formal agreement was drawn up to establish ties between the Nottinghamshire Army Cadet Force and the Barbados Cadet Corps.

Nottinghamshire's participation in our International Cadet Challenge Camp and a reciprocal visit by Barbadian cadets to the United Kingdom were part of the arrangement. Colonel Reynolds donated a trophy to mark the occasion. He hoped that it would be used for competitions within the Barbados Cadet Corps.

It was a dream realized and it was benefitting both Barbados and the Nottinghamshire ACF. With subsequent visits to Barbados, Col. Reynolds and I became very good friends. It was amazing the way bonds were formed through the military/Cadet Corps links we established.

With Major Terry Thacker and Mrs. Val Thacker.

Suffolk was the other British ACF targeted. As far back as 1998, while sitting at my desk, I was told that a British ACF Officer, Lieutenant Terry Thacker, was in the Clerk's office and wanted to meet me. I invited him to my office, where he showed me his identification card. His wife Val remained downstairs speaking with one of the Cadet Headquarters staff members. Her version of the story was that they were driving around the Garrison and Terry braked suddenly when he saw the sign marked "Barbados Cadet Corps Headquarters" and immediately turned into the driveway.

That was what I call "duty beyond the desk." He was on holiday, but was still ready to discuss possible links with the Barbados Cadet Corps. The true cadet corps officer is continually preoccupied with his cadets and their present and future well-being.

Terry and Val returned to Barbados the following year and made contact with me. This time, I instinctively invited them to our home. I did so knowing that my wife would join me in showing them the hospitality for which Barbadians are known.

Since then, they have visited Barbados every year and sometimes twice a year. We have spent a lot of time together, and we are like brothers and sisters.

Mrs. Val Thacker and my wife Eartha.

Terry and I often spoke about possible exchanges. I thought that if I went to the UK, I would be able to meet with their Commandant and headquarters personnel to build something lasting for the future.

Therefore, with Col. Reynolds in Nottinghamshire, and Major Terry Thacker in Suffolk, this trip offered great possibilities. Unfortunately it was not approved by the Barbados Defence Force Headquarters. Undaunted, I found an alternative plan.

Pete and Caroline with Major Glyne Grannum, Cmdr. Ricardo Shurland and myself in the BDF Officers'Mess.

I took vacation, and requested permission from the BDF to contact the British Army Cadet Forces in England. The members of the Barbados Cadet Association Inc. understood the importance of the visit, and assisted with the resources to make the trip successful.

Lieutenant Col. Riley at left of photo.

Life is about how you reach out to people and the selfless deeds one does simply in service to others. Earlier in 2010, Lieutenant Colonel Riley, who was also Chairman of the London Wing Air Training Corps Welfare Committee, told me that two friends, Flight Lieutenant and Media Officer Pete Gourri and his wife Caroline, a Squadron

Leader and the Media Officer for London and South East Region, would be holidaying in Barbados from May 28 to June 7.

When they contacted us, we arranged to collect them from their hotel and have lunch at our home. In London, they reciprocated by collecting me and my wife from the airport and taking us to their home for the first three days.

It was good to have met Pete and Caroline. We were on the verge of establishing an air cadet unit, and this gave me an opportunity to learn more about Air Cadets.

Arriving at Gatwick at 5:50 a.m., we were scheduled to be at Westminster Abbey at 10.00 a.m. for a service to mark a special anniversary of the Royal Air Force. We met Colonel Riley's wife and a daughter, whom we had met in Barbados a few months before. After the service, there was a march past and we had an opportunity to see the air cadets marching.

Eartha and I standing in front of Westminster Abbey.

Author Presenting Lieutenant Colonel Woods with a gift in appreciation of his assistance.

Staying at Pete's and Caroline's home allowed Lieutenant Colonel Riley to take me to various areas of interest. He met me at the train station, and we visited Frimley Park, the main cadet training centre, where I met with the Chief Instructor to discuss how the Barbados Cadet Corps could gain access to the training done there.

Lieutenant Colonel Riley also took me to his workplace, the Cadet Vocational Qualification Office. I learnt about the British system, where cadet training could qualify students for certificates equivalent to academic subjects. While there, I met Lieutenant Colonel Edward Woods who, along with Lieutenant Colonel Riley, had been exposing Caribbean cadets to this very beneficial programme. Finally, we went to the Royal Air Force Club to see how an air cadet corps could be developed in Barbados and what training opportunities existed.

An Air Cadet unit had been approved by our Defence Board. It was a project, in which Lieutenant Colonel Browne had put tremendous effort, and I would have liked to assist in setting up yet another unit, but my tour of duty has ended. I hope that the benefits of such a unit are fully understood by all and that they will continue to explore these links.

Author Presenting a mahogany clock in appreciation of the exchange between our two units.

Having completed the London leg of the visit, my Barbadian friends, Jim and Montel Birkett, came from Nottinghamshire to take us to their home. Jim was a cadet in No. 3 Company, who joined the British Army in the early 1960s. While in Nottinghamshire, Col. Reynolds took us to Nottinghamshire ACF Headquarters, where we met Commandant, Col. Nigel Rippon.

Barbadian and British cadets at camp in the UK

We had dinner with Col. Reynolds and Jane and stayed overnight in his home. He was immensely kind and made us feel at home.

The exchanges between the Barbados Cadet Corps and Nottinghamshire and Suffolk Army Cadet Forces were therefore on sound footing, and the Barbadian Cadets were well received in the United Kingdom.

Capt. Errol Brathwaite, the Contingent Commander to the United Kingdom, said that the trip to the UK was a success. He noted that Cadets were able to participate in a number of exciting activities. He felt that his cadets blended well with their peers from the Notts and Derby Army Cadet Forces.

I received an email from Colonel Nigel Rippon after our camp visit in 2011. Referring to our cadets he said:

> Patrick,
>
> It was my absolute pleasure to host your officers and cadets at our recent annual camp and I must say, they were all a credit to their Cadet Corps. Each and every one of them was very polite,immaculately turned out, very responsive, if not a little cold. I sincerely hope we gave them an experience they would never forget. We are already looking towards 2010.
>
> Col Rippon

Barbadian Cadets in London

Such reports made my day and gave me the motivation to continue. I was happy to have been able to work with the various authorities and my contacts in the United Kingdom to offer these cadets an opportunity to go beyond the Caribbean. Personal financial circumstances would have hindered many of them from undertaking such a trip.

Colonel Reynolds continued to be an inspiration. Between his visits to the Barbados Cadet Corps Headquarters and his assistance to us in the United Kingdom, he was also doing duty beyond the desk.

Next it was Terry and Val Thacker's turn to assist. They came to Nottinghamshire and took us to Norfolk, where we spent the last five days at their home. It was a pleasure to be with them and to finally meet their relatives and friends of whom we had heard so much over the past decade.

Terry arranged for me to visit the home of his Deputy Commandant, Lieutenant Colonel Bob West and the Suffolk Army Cadet Force Headquarters, where I also met the Cadet Executive Officer, Major Bob Potter. Major Potter was very helpful and even provided information I had requested on cadet safety regulations.

I did a presentation on the Barbados Cadet Corps and listened attentively as they presented their information on the Suffolk Army Cadet Force.

Officers and cadets of the Barbados Cadet Corps visited the United Kingdom as guests of the Suffolk Army Cadet Force in 2011 and 2012. Cadets from Suffolk were scheduled to pay a reciprocal visit to Barbados in 2013.

In 2011, Lieutenant Colonel Bob West and Major Terry Thacker came to Barbados on a recce, at their own expense, in anticipation of a possible

(L-R) Lt. Col. R. Vickers, Lt. Col. A. Branch, Lt. Col. T. Browne, Hon. R. Jones, Col. Alvin Quintyne, Lt. Col. Bob West (Suffolk ACF) Rev. M. Walfall (padre) Mrs. Eartha Skeete (partly hidden), Major P. Skeete.

Lt. Col. Bob West (extreme left) and Major Terry Thacker sharing a light-hearted moment with Lt. Cdr. Carl Farley (second from left) and Major James Bradshaw.

visit by their Cadets. Eartha and I accommodated them at our home, and we spent much time chatting and building our relationships.

While they were here, they engaged in a range of activities. These included a courtesy call on the Commandant of the Barbados Cadet Corps, Lt.Col. Trevor Browne; and visits to our campsite at Paragon and other locations where they observed our cadets in training.

The high point of their visit was their participation in a ceremony at the Lloyd Erskine Sandiford Centre. It was intended as a public relations event to educate parents and guardians about the benefits of the Cadet Corps. In attendance were the Minister of Education, the Hon. Ronald Jones; the Chief of Staff, Col. Alvin Quintyne; the Deputy Chief of Staff, Lt. Col. Atheline Branch; and the Commandant, Lt. Col. Trevor Browne, who presented Lt. Col. West with a token of appreciation. After presenting a commemorative plaque to Lt. Col. Browne, Lt. Col. West addressed the gathering of over one thousand guests.

Bob, Terry, Eartha and I enjoying a meal at a local restaurant.

Lieutenant Colonel West and Major Thacker were also invited to dinner at the British High Commissioner's residence. This was a very strong show of support of our efforts to form links with British Army Cadets Forces. In his remarks at dinner, Mr. Paul Brummel, the British High Commissioner, thanked us for the work we were doing to forge these ties. The Chief of Staff of the Barbados Defence Force also attended that event.

We made sure that our visitors saw as much of the island as possible and that they enjoyed a wide variety of local cuisine. Bob continues to speak of the wonderful time he spent in Barbados. Indeed, the entire experience resulted in lasting friendships and solid working relationships between the officers and cadets of both countries.

It is clear that the success of events for volunteer organizations is built largely on the social relationships between the key players. Systems alone cannot do it. The danger, however, is that when these key players leave, the enterprise could collapse. I have tried to avoid this by ensuring that officers have contact information. The hope is that by sending adult officers to overseas camps, there will be continuity.

However, it is important for all concerned to want to interact and keep in touch. That requires effort, and is part of one's duty beyond the desk. It is not prescribed. It has to come from the heart.

39

Rationale Behind Overseas Engagements

There was a very simple rationale behind all the overseas engagements. We noticed that during the summer vacation, many senior cadets were accepting summer jobs and not attending camp. This created challenges with training and supervision of cadets. As mentioned before, only one cadet per school could attend the Caribbean Cadet Camp, which became less attractive as a result. What was needed was a massive overseas camp campaign, much like what we achieved in the 1970s.

This was a very important strategy in the "retention" phase of our development, and within a short period of time, large numbers of senior cadets were returning to camp.

At one time, only cadets from schools with sixth forms (Harrison College, The Lodge School, Queen's College and Combermere School), were able to continue as cadets until the age of 19 years 11 months. Now, there was a new initiative where students from Tertiary institutions were allowed to be cadets until that same age. As a result, students were leaving secondary school and entering either the Barbados Community College, the Samuel Jackman Prescod Polytechnic or the University of the West Indies with the expectation of being able to continue to be cadets and be eligible to travel overseas. In the process, they were actively pursuing their higher education and it was therefore a win-win situation.

Unlike some of their counterparts in the Regular Force, Cadet Corps officers had limited exposure to training overseas. With only one officer a year attending a Caribbean camp and one Commandant and Staff Officer attending the Commandants' Conference, it would take several years before the average officer got an opportunity to travel overseas. With these overseas camps officers travelled more frequently. By successfully completing overseas engagements, we were not only strengthening our adult and cadet resources, we were also fulfilling the plans laid down in our Strategic Plan, 2001-2011.

Overseas Engagements in the Caribbean

One of the goals of our Strategic Plan was to form links with international cadet corps. We played a significant role in the Caribbean, having attended all the Caribbean Camps and Caribbean Commandants' Conferences. We collaborated with the St. Vincent Cadet Force to create a Strategic Development Plan for the Caribbean Cadet Association in St. Lucia in 2009, and helped establish cadet corps in the Cayman Islands and the British Virgin Islands in 2002 and 2009 respectively. We also sent Star 4 cadets on a mission to Tortola in 2009 to work with their new cadets at Star 1 level.

We conducted train-the-trainers' programmes in Dominica (2007) and St. Vincent (2008), funded by the United Nations Development Programme and the Barbados Cadet Association Inc. respectively.

We also assisted with the revival of the Grenada Cadet Corps by sending forty-eight cadets to serve as role models for the new cadets, revise the Star 1 syllabus and conduct examinations.

Through helping others, our personnel at both the adult and cadet levels gained valuable experience and were able to fine-tune their skills. By 2010, we had thirty-three master cadets, whereas in 2007 there were fifteen. Similarly, forty-eight Star 4 cadets went to Grenada, while in 2007 only twenty-five went to Dominica.

Undoubtedly, this effort motivated our cadets and enhanced the image of the Barbados Cadet Corps overseas. In so doing, it also enhanced the image of Barbados as a whole.

International Engagements

We developed the link with Canada, and the visits by the Director and the first group of Canadians showed the extent to which we had achieved our objective. In addition, our Corps had established links with two British Army Cadet Forces and there were prospects for links with air and sea cadets from the United Kingdom.

Our three main goals were recruiting, retention and leadership training. These overseas engagements helped significantly in these areas. These activities also had significant implications for tourism.

This summarizes the thinking process which drove the Commandant and me. It is important to share this information so that future leaders can understand why they have a responsibility to seek out new and exciting prospects for the Corps.

40

Key Ingredients for Successful Management

Money and resources do not guarantee that an organization will function effectively. They are important, but so is harmonious leadership.

The strength of my relationship with Lt. Col. Browne grew from our tendency to spend long hours discussing the business of the Cadet Corps. Early in our association, we made two important decisions. First, we agreed that if we wanted other interest groups to support us, then we needed to do everything at the highest standard possible. We also decided that we would not allow lack of funds to be a hindrance. This was where the Barbados Cadet Association Inc. and other support groups like the British Women's Club became vital. Groups such as the Barbados Workers' Union offered the use of its facilities instead of money. Their help allowed us to provide services to the cadets, which might not have been possible through public funding.

I must mention Mr. Bill Blackman, a former cadet from No.1 Company and founding member of the Barbados Cadet Association Inc. This Association comprised former cadets, who started a company with their own money to help the Cadet Corps.

Bill and I became very dear friends. He visited the Cadet Headquarters almost daily, and was a tremendous source of inspiration for me. His passion for "cadetting" sometimes outshone that of others who were fully integrated into the cadet system. I will be eternally grateful to him and his colleagues, who responded whenever a request was made for assistance.

We budgeted carefully, and our resources grew over the eighteen years of my tenure. Our development was also evident in the number of local and overseas camps held. As far as possible, Lieutenant Colonel Browne avoided using public funds for his overseas visits. He preferred that the funds be used for the cadets, and on a few occasions, he donated personal funds to pay for tickets for cadets to travel overseas. Such was the level of commitment and the nature of Lieutenant Colonel Trevor Browne.

There were significant inputs made by the Barbados Government, the Barbados Defence Force, Principals, parents and support groups such as the Multinational Women's Forum, the British Women's Club, the Barbados Workers Union, the Royal Barbados Police Band, the Barbados Cadet Association Inc. and others. However, the real secret to success of the last ten exciting years lies in the ***harmonious relationship*** between the Commandant and me, in the ***extraordinary efforts put in by Cadet Corps officers*** above and beyond the call of duty, and in the ***dedication exhibited by former cadets like Mr. Bill Blackman***, which fueled our progress during those very productive years.

41

Mourning With Our Cadets

I have recounted mostly happy times, but life is often full of ups and downs and we have to learn to cope with all eventualities.

During the last seven years of my career, there had been at least one death of a cadet per year. These deaths, though unrelated to activities in the Corps, were extremely taxing and emotionally draining.

The Officer Commanding the unit would call me, as Cadet Executive Officer, to say that one of his cadets had died. With that knowledge, I would first notify the Cadet Commandant and then the Barbados Defence Force Headquarters.

Working through the Officer Commanding, who would have known the family, we would make arrangements to visit the parents or guardians as early as possible. I was usually accompanied by the BDF padre, most recently, the Rev. Esther Willoughby.

In visiting these households, we always heard how much the deceased loved the Cadet Corps and how much it had influenced their lives. This discussion often brought smiles to very sorrowful faces. These were bitter sweet moments. I often sat and listened as parents recounted instances which showed the fervor with which their children approached their cadet activities. I felt very proud to be associated with this outstanding organization.

We recognized that it was our responsibility to do as much as possible to assist the family in their moment of bereavement. The real challenge came at the funeral where the cadets would have to face up to the loss of a comrade. It was not only the students from the late cadet's school, but a wider group, who felt the pain and sadness. Cadets normally train in Star Level groups during the year and at camps and, as a result, friendships develop between students from different schools. The death of one cadet touched many cadets.

I was amazed at how well the cadets performed their duties; handing wreaths to senior officers, blowing the bugle and lining the pathway. At one of the funerals, I once passed a cadet with tears streaming down his cheeks, but standing erect at attention nevertheless. Mr. Bill Blackman, who was walking behind me, later explained that a lady who was passing this said cadet walked over and dried his tears knowing that he could not flinch. That moment has remained etched in my mind.

Sometimes the emotions were too great for some of the cadets, and they would lean on each other for support. These were all valuable lessons in coping with the loss of a loved one.

Through our handling of these tragic circumstances, we made the parents of cadets aware that as long as you were a cadet, we would always be there to offer support in good and bad times.

42

Savouring Retirement

Days before I submitted my letter of retirement, I notified my family, the Cadet Commandant, my Pastor and all the important people in my life. When I submitted the letter, I was determined to make it final, and therefore felt an immediate responsibility to inform the Barbados Cadet Corps officers and the staff at Cadet Headquarters. News travels quickly and I did not want them to hear about my retirement second hand. I was content to put pen to paper, knowing that this was one letter where I would not have to worry over whether or not permission would be granted.

That same evening, I informed my overseas contacts, including regional Commandants and my friends in Canada and the United Kingdom.

Responding to my email about my retirement, my friend Colonel Clinton Riley said, in part,

> Dear Patrick, shocked would be an understatement! What can I say you are going to be a very hard act to follow and you have set the bar high for your successor? Just looking back over your CV you can be very proud of your achievements with the Barbados Cadet Corps, not

only that but the dedicated personal work that you have given to the Young People of Barbados through the Cadet Experience. I also feel that you can reflect on the support you have provided to the other Cadet Corps who are part of the Caribbean Cadet Association they have a lot to thank you for. Your vision to extend that experience to the Cadet Exchanges to Countries such as the UK has opened up a whole new World for the Young People not only in Barbados but also the UK.

I have been immensely impressed with your energy and dedication to the Cadet Forces and you can look back with great pride. The fact that Rihanna, who is an international celebrity still speaks in interviews about how she benefited from the Barbados Cadet Experience is a great credit to you and the Cadet Corps.

I think you can also be proud of how respected you are in the World of the International Cadet Forum and I know here that many people always speak highly of you in conversation from the early days of exchanges by Mark Andrews and James Morris to Barbados to the more recent exchanges with Nottingham
and Suffolk ACF.

Keep me informed of developments and I understand that Edward will be coming out to the Conference in July.

Clinton

His sentiments touched my heart.

Nevertheless, tributes fade. With each passing milestone, experiences drift further back into one's mind, only to become memories. If these memories are written down, they might endure and inspire some young person seeking direction in life.

After all the long, hard hours, I look forward to being at home, basking in the love and support of my dear wife Eartha, enjoying her company even more.

As a father and a grandfather, I still have an opportunity to walk closely with my children and grandchildren, and give them all the support they need. I have already mentioned Gemma, Alicia and Janelle from my first marriage and Gemma's son Joel. I have a stepdaughter, Keitha, from my marriage to Eartha and a stepson, Earthon, whose children are my grandchildren, and will also need guidance.

With My wife Eartha.

As a Deacon of the Berean Bible Church, I use my skills as part of my ministry for the Lord. I was glad to have met our Pastor Ronald Trotman years ago. I truly admired his sincerity, his humility, his genuine desire to help others and, most importantly, the example he set as a leader of the church. It was always good to meet someone who lives by what they preach.

Through his teachings, the role which I played in life and the new roles, which I am being called to fulfill, become clearer to me. We are accountable to God for our actions, but we have to be careful that when we do good deeds, we do not think that that is enough. We do good work and help others, and sometimes we conclude that that is what Christianity is about. But we forget that it is only through accepting Jesus as our Saviour and living according to His Word that we can truly say that we are Christians.

Divine providence and trust in the Lord have played a great role in my life. Now it is time to do His work.

I enjoy the fellowship at the Berean Church. I also think it was a blessing that I met my wife in a church environment - the church where we got married. Certainly, beyond the desk here at Cadet Headquarters, there is still much work to be done, and I will play my part in that regard.

The Inter-School/Intervarsity Christian Fellowship needs as much support as possible and so does the Child Evangelism Fellowship. As a member of the Boards of both organizations, I will try to ensure that as many students as possible have an opportunity to know God and make Him known.

So, what else am I going to do now? I am going to take a long vacation where I will no longer have to seek formal permission to go on leave. I look forward to the wonderful opportunity to relax without deadlines, pressure of work and the "stresses and strains" which can sometimes accompany a job. It is important to know when to withdraw. Timing is of the essence.

43 The Finale

The curtain call resounds backstage. I must answer that call and bow graciously before the audience, in appreciation of their support. My life's story will again take center stage.

There were a few major challenges with which I struggled, and some issues which were easily overcome because they were within our control. However, there were other challenges which only the authorities could rectify, including the status of Cadet Corps/BDF Officers and the inability to recruit large numbers of officers. These issues will have a significant effect in a few years when many of us have retired. But these are matters for my replacement to tackle. Perhaps, he will be more successful in this regard.

It is time now to stop daydreaming. In a few minutes, I will be going downstairs to attend a farewell function which my staff is holding for me in the Colonel Cooper Room.

I was asked to say who I wanted there. I specifically wanted to share the moment with officers from the Corps and former staff members from Cadet Headquarters. These were people with whom I worked closely over the years and I wanted them to know that I appreciated their company, support and assistance.

Not long ago, the Commandant, Lieutenant Colonel Browne, in collaboration with the Barbados Cadet Association Inc., arranged a special farewell ceremony at The Lloyd Erskine Sandiford Centre. I had spent my entire career reaching out to various partners and I wanted these groups to be represented. I wanted my wife, children and extended family to be present to share this experience with me.

This official function at The Lloyd Erskine Sandiford Centre was a grand affair. The Deputy High Commissioner of the United Kingdom, Mr. Phil Culligan, was there, as were the Canadian High Commissioner, Her Excellency Ruth Archibald and the Deputy Chief of Staff, Lt. Col. Atheline Branch. Retired BDF officers who were present included the former

Being presented with a plaque by The Hon. Stephen Lashley while my wife and family look on.

Deputy Chief of Staff, Commander Wilbert Kirton, former Deputy Chief of Staff, Lt. Col. Florence Gittens, Lt. Col. John Nurse and Lt. Col. Jeffrey Bostic. The British Women's Club was represented and so too were the Barbados Workers' Union and the Combermere Old Scholars Association. I was particularly happy to see the present Principal, Mr. Vere Parris, and former Principals of Combermere School.

My cousin Marva, who helped to look after me as a baby while my mother was doing her needle work, was there along with parents and cadets. Also present in the audience were friends of my wife, church members and representatives of the Inter-School-Inter-Varsity Christian Fellowship.

The Minister of Youth, The Hon. Stephen Lashley, himself a former cadet, gave the feature address.

The British High Commissioner, Mr. Paul Brummell, later sent me an email explaining that he was not in Barbados at the time of the ceremony. In his email, he said, among other things, "Can I record my thanks for your great work and dedication in building links between the Cadet Corps in Barbados and their opposite numbers in the United Kingdom, and wish you a long and happy retirement?"

Guests at author's retirement function.

I was not aware that my work had had such an impact at that level.

It was truly a nostalgic moment. There is just this one last activity to face. I had planned so many events to congratulate, honour and thank people in the past. Now the roles have been reversed. I am now on the receiving end. But before I leave this room, I must regain my composure, hold back the emotions and try to get through this last one.

Appreciation

I wish to thank the following:

The Archives Department for their assistance over the years as I did research into the history of the Barbados Cadet Corps.

The Barbados Defence Force for allowing me to use photos of Cadet activities.

My colleagues of the Cadet Corps/Forces of the Caribbean, Canada and the United Kingdom for agreeing to the use of photos of their Cadet units.

Colonel (ret'd) Deighton Maynard for assisting with proofreading and for contributing the Foreword.

Grafixx 2 Inc for the meticulous work done on the cover design and general layout of the book.

Ms Sandra Reid for editing the book.

13691777R00124

Printed in Great Britain
by Amazon.co.uk, Ltd.,
Marston Gate.